COMPETITION
CARRIAGE DRIVING

COMPETITION CARRIAGE DRIVING

HRH THE DUKE of EDINBURGH

J.A. ALLEN: LONDON

British Library Cataloguing in Publication Data
A catalogue record for this book is available from the
British Library.

ISBN 0.85131.594.1

First published in 1982 by Horse Drawn
Carriages Limited.
This revised edition published in 1994 by

J.A. Allen & Company Limited,
1 Lower Grosvenor Place, Buckingham Palace Road,
London, SW1W 0EL.

Typeset in Hong Kong by Setrite Typesetters Ltd
Printed in Spain by Printeksa
Edited by Elizabeth O'Beirne-Ranelagh

Designed by Paul Saunders

Frontispiece. HRH The Duke of Edinburgh negotiates the water at Windsor with the competition team of HM The Queen's bays. *(Author's Collection)*

CONTENTS

PREFACE TO SECOND EDITION

As you will see in the Introduction, the first FEI Rules for Carriage Driving Competitions were issued in 1969. I started competing in 1973 and the first edition of this book came out in 1982. Things changed fairly drastically in the first ten years and they have changed even more in the last ten years. While the basic concept of the competition is much the same – it remains based on the ridden three-day event formula – some quite radical changes have had to be made in the light of experience. In this edition I have corrected the text to take account of the changes, but otherwise it remains very much as it was first written.

The two most significant changes to the rules in recent years have been the dropping of 'Presentation' as a separate competition, and the introduction of a scoring system for the hazards based entirely on the time taken by competitors to negotiate a hazard from the moment they enter the 'in' flags until they leave the 'out' flags. This has also made it possible to do away with penalty zones, which always caused problems for the hazard judges.

The biggest change for me came in 1986 when I retired from the horse teams class after the World Championships at Ascot, but I did not retire from driving altogether. I had already been competing occasionally with a team of Fell ponies for some years, so the transfer was not quite as drastic as it might seem. Quite a few people have moved from pony teams to horse teams, and I suspect that this is a more difficult move, but I know of no one else who has gone from horses to ponies. They suit me because ponies are a lot smaller and take up much less room in the hazards, they are more nimble and, once you can get the Fells enthused, they are quicker at starting and, usually, stopping. As their centre of gravity is that much lower than horses, it should be possible to turn them more sharply at speed. After thirteen years' competing with horses, including a fair number of championships and other events abroad, I find the pony teams class rather more light-hearted and it has provided me with a great deal of fun. Furthermore, most of the other pony team drivers are considerably more glamorous than our colleagues in the horse teams class.

Since the first edition was published, the number of competitors in most of the eight classes has continued to grow and the number of events has grown with them. Equally important is that the number of experienced officials of all kinds and organisers of events has also increased. This has meant a great improvement in the general management of events and there are far fewer organisational problems and hiccups. The major problem is finding sponsorship. The recession has taken its toll of willing sponsors for both events and drivers, while the costs of the sport have certainly not diminished.

The biggest advance in the organisation of events has been the improvement in hazard design. No course designer will ever please everyone, but they have learned a great deal over the years and the quality of their designs improves all the time.

On the technical side, having tried and rejected the 'bendy carriage' idea, we now have the 'bendy pole'. This is probably the most radical innovation since the turn-table was invented. The idea originated on the continent and was kept a closely guarded secret for a time, until British drivers suspected that something funny was going on and eventually discovered the system. It is a completely new invention for carriages and, while it works very well when it works, the engineering design still needs to be perfected.

INTRODUCTION

Driving horses and ponies has been growing in popularity since the 1950s, but it was only when the International Equestrian Federation (FEI) published the first set of international rules for driving competitions in 1969 that competitive driving began to develop in Britain.

The purpose of this book is to pass on what experience I have gained of this type of competition in the hope that it will help newcomers to the sport to avoid some of the trials and tribulations which I had to learn the hard way. But, first of all, it might be useful to put down how it all started.

Like many things, it all began with a casual conversation. I had been elected president of the FEI in 1964 in spite of the fact that my only equestrian activity had been on the polo field. As it happened this turned out to be quite fortunate, because while I knew enough about horses and riding to understand what they were all talking about, I was able to be a neutral chairman between the dressage, jumping and three-day event factions in the Federation. Anyway, at one of the annual general assemblies I found myself talking to Eric Brabec, one of the Polish delegates, and he suggested that the FEI ought to produce some international rules for driving competitions.

My first reaction was somewhat sceptical. The only sort of driving I had ever seen were those coaching classes at some British horse shows, and classes organised by the British Driving Society, and their drives did not strike me as a likely basis for an international competition. However, having had so many of my own brilliant ideas turned down at various times, I had made up my mind long ago that I would never turn anything down unless it was patently absurd. As I didn't know whether there was anything in this idea I thought I had better find out. I soon discovered that there were indeed a number of thriving four-in-hand dressage and cross-country trial type driving competitions on the continent, and although several of them, such as Hamburg, were 'international' in that competitors from other countries were taking part, each had its own set of rules. I then paid a visit to the Aachen Horse Show where I saw twenty-four four-in-hand teams, mainly German and Hungarian, driving round the ring and it became very obvious that the idea was worth pursuing.

The next move was dictated by two incidents which had taken place some years earlier. Sir Michael Ansell had been a regular guest at Badminton House for the horse trials and it was as a result of a conversation with him one evening after dinner that he started the Pony Club Mounted Games. That was the first incident; the second occurred when I was invited to stand for president of the FEI. As Sir Michael was already a member of the Bureau (Executive Committee) of the FEI, I naturally turned to him for advice. He persuaded me to accept.

Here, I thought, was an ideal opportunity to make use of his organising talents and to get my own back on him at the same time, so I asked him to chair an international committee to produce some international rules for driving competitions. When I put this to him he thought I was joking and protested that he knew nothing about driving, but when I explained the situation to him and pointed out that he didn't seem to object to my being president of the FEI in spite of my ignorance of its three disciplines, and that he was a senior member of the Bureau as well as liked and respected throughout the equestrian world, he readily agreed to have a try. Anybody who has ever worked with Mike Ansell knows what he was like when he wanted

to get something done. He wasted no time in scooping up all the people in Europe who knew about driving, brought them together in Berne, worked them till all hours and returned with an agreed outline for a competition based on the ridden three-day event. I doubt whether anyone else could have done it.

After that things began to happen rather too quickly for my liking. Rules are notoriously difficult things to get right and all we had were a few typewritten pages and absolutely no experience, no judges, no organisers, no time-keepers and no course designers, but none of this deterred the Swiss Federation from proposing to organise in 1970 the first international competition in Lucerne using the new rules.

It so happened that Sir John Miller, then The Queen's Crown Equerry, and in charge of the Royal Mews, was a very keen driving man and I knew that he had taken to driving four-in-hands from the Buckingham Palace Mews. I therefore suggested that he might be interested to have a go at this competition and to let me know what he thought of it. Many of the subsequent improvements and refinements to the rules are due to his practical experience in those early years.

Things kept going at an alarming pace. After a bit of arm twisting the Windsor Horse Show put on an international driving competition for four-in-hands in 1971 and in the autumn of the same year the Hungarians organised the first European Championships. The Windsor competition has continued annually and European and World Championships have alternated ever

since, and in 1980 the World Championships took place in Windsor Great Park with forty-two entries from eleven countries, which compares quite favourably with the Championships in the other disciplines.

My own original involvement was due entirely to the fact that I was president of the FEI but it so happened that I had decided to give up polo in 1970 – I reckoned that fifty was quite old enough for that game – and I was looking around for something else to do, in what little leisure time I seemed to have. It soon became apparent that this driving business might be just the thing. Horses, carriages, coachmen and grooms were all available in the Mews and, provided I stuck to the horses that were usable and available for State occasions, there would be little extra cost involved either for myself or for the Mews.

In 1971 I went to Budapest to watch the first European Championships. In 1972 I went round the Windsor course as referee with the

Lieutenant Colonel Sir John Miller, the Crown Equerry from 1961 to 1987, taking part in the Presentation phase of the European Championships, 1975, at Sopot, Poland. He is driving a Beaufort Phaeton to a team of four of HM The Queen's horses comprising two greys, Rio and Santiago, and two bays, Eagle and Kestrel. *(Author's Collection)*

HRH The Duke of Edinburgh refereeing Sandor Fülop, Royal Windsor Horse Show, 1972. (*Hulton Deutsch*)

(*below*) A team of Her Majesty The Queen's bays at the State Opening of Parliament, November 1980. These horses were used by HRH The Duke of Edinburgh in competition (see frontispiece). (*PR London District*)

Hungarian, Sandor Fülop, and in January 1973 Sir John Miller let me have five bays from the Royal Mews, and I trained myself and them at Sandringham with the help of Major 'Tommy' Thompson. I was exceptionally fortunate to have Major Thompson. He had recently retired as Riding Master of the Household Cavalry, he was an experienced coaching whip and he had ridden in a number of three-day events including Badminton from 1949 to 1953.

My first competition was at Lowther in April 1973 and the second was at the Windsor Horse

HRH The Duke of Edinburgh driving the team of Fell ponies which he now competes with in the dressage test at Stanmer Park, Brighton. *(Alf. Baker)*

Show a month later which, as luck would have it, was also the European Championships. Sadly I hit the last of the eight hazards on the cross-country and had to retire with a bent carriage, but I did manage a clear round through the cones and another clear round in the drive-off. I should add that the carriage I used for the marathon was a splendidly old-fashioned vehicle known as the 'Balmoral Dogcart'. In present-day conditions it would be hopelessly unsuitable.

Since then the rules have undergone a number of minor changes but the competition is still essentially based on the ideas put forward by Sir Michael Ansell and his committee at their historic meeting in Berne in June 1969.

The Balmoral Dogcart.
(*Alf. Baker*)

CHAPTER 1

THE FEI RULES FOR DRIVING EVENTS

The first and basic essential requirement for anyone wishing to participate in any sport is to know the rules. This may sound obvious but it is surprising how many people do not know the rules or who think they know the rules.

The FEI publishes the Rules for Driving Events in English and French as a booklet in a brown cover in the same style and layout as the Rules for Jumping, Dressage and Three-day Events. A new edition is published every four years and only minor changes or corrections can be made during the four-year period the edition is in force. Competitors are highly recommended to acquire a personal copy as well as a copy of the British National Rules.

The introduction to the Rules (Article 900) sets out the purpose:

These rules are not intended to standardise driving competitions, but international competitions must be strictly fair to all com-

petitors. It is therefore necessary to lay down a number of strict and comprehensive rules, which must be carefully observed. At the same time, within these rules organising committees have the right to use their discretion to make their Events interesting for the competitors and attractive for the spectators.

Article 901, paragraph 1, states:

These rules provide for three types of competitions:
Competition A – Dressage
Competition B – Marathon
Competition C – Obstacle Driving

A combination of any of these will be known as a Combined Driving Competition.

There is little point in quoting any more from the Rules as they are liable to change, but drivers should have particular regard to Chapter II 'Conditions', Chapter IV 'Classification' and then Chapters V, VI and VII which deal with

'Dressage', 'The Marathon' and 'The Obstacle Driving Test' respectively. All the Appendices are worth reading, particularly those which deal with the dressage tests as the tests have to be learned by heart.

You will notice that the scoring system is almost exactly the same as that used by the ridden three-day event. In other words, penalty points are given in each competition and these are added together to give the final score, the competitor with the lowest score naturally being the winner.

In the first edition of the Rules the obstacles on the marathon were referred to as hazards, to distinguish them from the obstacles or cones used in Competition C 'Obstacle Driving'. The word was dropped in later editions in favour of the word 'obstacles' because there is no appropriate equivalent to the word 'hazard' in French. However, in order to avoid confusion I shall use the term 'hazard' for the obstacles in the marathon competition and 'obstacles' for those in the obstacle driving competition.

CHAPTER 2

HORSES

———•———

With a few minor differences the rules apply equally to singles, pairs, tandems and teams of ponies or horses so that there is obviously a very wide choice of what to drive. Strangely enough, and contrary to what might be supposed, it does not follow that the more animals you drive, the more difficult things become. It may be easier to drive a single than a pair, and easier to drive a pair than a team, but that does not mean to say that you will automatically get better marks in the competition with a single or a pair. In fact, I believe that a competent driver can produce a better dressage test with a team than he can with a pair or a single. Provided the team is physically and temperamentally well matched, they tend to even out the minor discrepancies and turn in a more flowing performance. I have not tried to compete with a tandem, but I would estimate that it is the most difficult combination; in fact I believe that it is a form of masochism!

The clue, of course, is the temperament of the animal or animals coupled with the competence and temperament of the driver. Unless driver and driven are compatible and confident in each other there is little hope of doing well in any of the competitions.

The difficulty is that the driver has got to make himself compatible with whatever he is driving and to do that he has to understand the character of his animals. Not only do animals of the same breed differ in individual characteristics but there is also a major difference between the attitudes and responses of ponies and horses.

Let no one believe that ponies are easier to drive than horses. What ponies lack in size they make up for in independence and speed of reaction. If anything goes wrong in driving it happens extremely quickly, but with ponies it is not only quick but usually unexpected and original – and frequently entirely irrational.

The fascinating thing about this competition is that each phase requires something special. In the dressage the animals need to be subtle, obedient and co-operative, and the driver needs to be patient, accurate and calm; for the marathon they need to be fit, strong, bold and hopefully intelligent, and the driver needs to be a careful planner with quick reactions; for the obstacles they need to be well co-ordinated, disciplined and calm and so does the driver. Put all these qualities together and you have an ideal competition horse and driver – that is, of course, if they are both in the right mood on the day. Furthermore, while the horse has to be fit and raring to go across country on the marathon it has to be manageable in the dressage test which takes place first. To get four such paragons in the hands of a competent driver at the same time is little short of miraculous.

As far as size is concerned, in theory at least, the ideal would be the smallest horses for the horse classes or the largest ponies for the pony classes. This is simply because bigger horses take up more room in the hazards and obstacles and the smaller the horse the smaller the carriage needs to be, although all horse-drawn four-in-hand carriages for the cross-country have to weigh at least 600 kg (300 kg for ponies). On the other hand very small ponies may have to swim the water crossings and very small carriages give a rough ride and are more difficult to pull. However, theory is not always a good guide and four big amenable horses will do better than four little tearaways. Equally, Shetland ponies are extremely tough, and seem to have exactly the right temperament for this sort of competition. In my opinion they are infinitely better at pulling a carriage than carrying small children on their backs.

The following are my impressions of the ponies that I have seen competing:

Shetland Tough, remarkably fast, intelligent and willing but, like so many pony breeds, they have a mind of their own and when it is made up it takes more than most drivers have got to change it. While they can compete with ponies twice their size in the marathon and the obstacles, their very smallness is a problem in the dressage.

Welsh Always good looking, good paces and full of going, but can be a bit mercurial in character, and inclined to boil over under stress or tension.

Exmoor Business-like and determined, but lacking perhaps the 'presence' of the Welsh.

Fell Tough, and extremely willing with plenty of speed. If anything, a bit dour in character, but the good ones are quite unflappable (see illustration, page 21).

Haflinger Very tough but need encouragement to develop speed. Very clever, in fact they can be too clever by half and are easily bored, although they respond to a challenge. Great independence of character.

Norwegian Fjord Strong and willing with a good turn of speed. In character they seem to be more like horses than ponies. They hold themselves well and have good paces.

The team of Cleveland Bays at Windsor, portrayed by B. R. Linklater, 1976.

Hackney Pony Bred to provide a really smart and flashy turn-out. They have everything needed for this competition, but they sometimes have too much of a good thing. Provided they have not seen too much of the show ring, they seem to settle down with experience.

Many of the horses used for driving are known as 'warmbloods' and are usually the product of native breeds crossed with thoroughbreds. There are few of the traditional native breeds of Europe that have not been subject to the infusion of thoroughbred or other blood in recent years, but stud-books are maintained for most of the following breeds:

Oldenburg Very big with probably the best paces of any of the carriage breeds. Fast and intelligent but their legs are inclined to be suspect. The problem is that they come in many shapes and sizes so that selection is important.

Gelderlander There have been many good Gelderland teams, but they have not been as successful in these competitions as might be expected. Inclined to carry their heads high and although they do a lot of work they don't seem to cover the ground. Dutch bred horses, probably with Gelderland blood, have done well, although their temperament seems to vary.

Friesian Powerful stocky horses rather like large Fell ponies but somewhat lacking in stamina and speed.

Hanoverian, Holstein Different breeds but very similar in conformation and temperament. Classic carriage horses, a bit on the large side, but with training and experience they can do very well, particularly in dressage.

Polish (Trakehner) Probably the best looking of the North German/Polish breeds and consistent performers in international competitions. The problem is to get good ones out of the Polish State Studs. Although there are Trakehner studs in other countries, the Polish bred horses are more the carriage type while the others have been selected more for riding.

Silesian The only ones I have seen are bred in Poland. In conformation more like a small black Suffolk Punch, but they certainly hold their own in competitions.

Hungarian Much the most successful in competition over the years, fast and amenable, but rather lacking in character. Not a true breed, although they have a distinctive rather 'leggy'

look about them, as they can include native, thoroughbred, trotter and possibly Lipizzaner blood.

Lipizzaner Bred as carriage horses and for high school work with a good temperament, in theory they should be ideal for competition work. The Hungarian driver, and former World Champion, Györgi Bardos was consistently successful with this breed.

Kladrub A very large Czechoslovak cousin of the Lipizzaner. Remarkably handy and amenable for such enormous horses.

Cleveland Bay Apart from Welsh Cobs and Hackney Horses, the only true British carriage horse. Powerful with great stamina and a generous temperament but lacking in paces, looks and speed. Probably better crossed either with a thoroughbred or an Oldenburg to give better paces and speed (see illustration, page 19).

Welsh Cob Ideal in size, speed and paces, but temperamentally a bit mercurial. Cobs have been consistently successful in driving competitions, provided the driver can hold them.

Hackney Horse Bred for speed, endurance, and presence, they should be the ideal breed for this competition and they have done very well, but as with the ponies, they can be too much of a good thing.

Morgan Purpose-bred as carriage horses in

North America, these strong, active and very fast trotters have proved to be well-suited to driving competitions.

Apart from these rather distinctive breeds there are a number of countries that breed what might be termed general purpose horses, and by judicious selection it is possible to put together a matching team. Swedish, Danish, Westphalian, Swiss, French and Austrian horses are among those which come under this heading but it is rather a gamble as matching conformation does not necessarily mean matching paces or temperaments. However, this can

HRH The Duke of Edinburgh with the team of Fell ponies at Windsor, portrayed by the artist B. R. Linklater. In the background is Karen Bassett's team of spotted ponies.

sometimes be turned to advantage by using high stepping Cobs in the wheel and the flowing toe pointing action of Hungarians in the lead. Another solution is to cross breed in the hope of getting the best characteristics of the two breeds. There is, of course, the equal chance that the progeny will inherit the worst characteristics of their parents.

The choice of competition horses or ponies depends on a number of factors, most of which are personal to the individual owner. If there is complete freedom of choice, perhaps a good way to set about it is to go to a major national driving event where most of the pony breeds will be represented and to an international event where most of the horse breeds can be seen in action. A team of matched horses of a particular breed gives a very good indication of the breed as a whole.

The only general advice I would offer is that it is not worth persisting with any animal that shows a consistent flaw in its temperament or quite obviously does not enjoy competitive driving. Some characteristics or bad habits can be cured, but by no means all of them, and there is no hope of establishing that essential bond of trust and confidence with an animal you simply do not like or trust.

CHAPTER 3

BRIDLES AND BITS

Harness and two-wheeled carriages for single ponies and horses is a whole subject in itself and I don't propose to deal with it in this book if only because I have no personal experience of driving singles.

The most important item in any harness is the bridle and bit. No matter how much they may look alike, no two horses have quite the same shape and size of head and even if they are very similar it is almost certain that their mouths will be different. This may be self-evident to a rider, but then a rider is only dealing with one horse at a time. The point is that whether driving a pair or a team each animal has to be treated as an individual.

The bit problem is difficult enough in a riding horse where both the mouth and temperament of the horse and the hands and temperament of the rider have to be taken into consideration. Much the same applies in driving but with the added problem that the driver cannot use his legs as aids to get his horses to go up to their bits. Voice and whip have to take the place of

legs and spurs, but obviously they act in a different way. The other difference is that allowance has to be made for the fact that a driver has to cope with up to four different mouths and temperaments at the same time.

The obvious difference between a riding bridle and a driving bridle is that the driving bridle is fitted with blinkers. There are various reasons for fitting blinkers but the most important is that it prevents the horses, particularly the wheelers, from seeing the whip being moved about. You cannot use the whip without moving it even if you just want to touch a wheeler, and you have to move it if you want to signal a turn or to blow your nose, or simply when handling the reins in a tight corner. The important point, therefore, is to see that the blinkers are attached and fitted in such a way that neither do they blind the horse, nor flap open so far that they are ineffective, and that they are not bigger than absolutely necessary. In the wild, the only way that horses can defend themselves against attack is by running away. The eyes of a horse are, therefore, so positioned that they can look behind them without turning their heads. The smallest gap between the blinker and the side of the head is quite enough for a horse to see what is going on behind it, and a nervous horse seems able to see a waving whip through the narrowest chink. On the other hand, if you are going to ask horses to find their way between trees, posts and rails, and plastic cones, it seems only reasonable to give them a chance to see where they are going. It doesn't help matters if they are constantly bumping into things because they can't see them. So, for the marathon and the obstacles, I put the leaders in cup-shaped blinkers (such as are sometimes fitted to race-horses), instead of the conventional variety. These give the leaders a wider field of view forwards and sideways while shielding their view of a waving whip behind them.

I have sometimes driven a complete team of Fell ponies in open bridles, but it depends on the temperament of the wheelers. I usually leave the leaders in open bridles and fit cup blinkers to the wheelers. I have to say that it is not a practice that has been readily adopted by other drivers, although I have seen a few teams of horses at international competitions with the leaders in open bridles, but it is a rare sight.

The basic rules about bridles is that they should fit the head and that the bits should lie comfortably in the mouth. The choice of the type of bit suitable for each individual horse is an art in itself but in general terms the bit should not be bigger, heavier or more severe than absolutely necessary, bearing in mind that a horse's mouth develops and matures with use and experience. Over-bitting can prevent a horse doing its work properly while under-bitting allows it to become unmanageable. However, never forget that the driver's temperament, strength and hands at the other end of the reins must also be taken into consideration.

One of the problems about driving, which does not occur in riding, is that in pairs and teams two horses are expected to go along side by side doing the same amount of work and doing it amicably. Needless to say this is an ideal state of affairs which does not always happen in practice. For some mysterious reason the wheel horses seldom nag each other; it may happen occasionally but not consistently. Leaders on the other hand can be persistent naggers and it is a most aggravating habit. There are several ways of dealing with the problem but none of them can guarantee success. A martingale can help by preventing a nagger from getting its head up high enough to get a bite at its neighbour and this, coupled with a dropped noseband to keep its mouth shut, sometimes works. Another possible treatment is the Abbot-Davis balancing rein or an ordinary bearing rein. Although they are intended for different purposes, in the case of a nagging horse they have the same effect of making it more difficult for a horse to turn its head to get at its neighbour. Unfortunately they can also have the effect of

(opposite, above left) 'Cup' blinkers. *(opposite, above right)* Noseband. *(opposite, below)* Martingale. *(Author's Collection)*

making a driven horse drop back from the bit, particularly if it otherwise has a good mouth.

In my opinion the most effective treatment is to tie a piece of stout string or washing line to the outside of the bit or bridle of the offending horse and lead it back through the terrets to the hand of a groom. A sharp twitch on the string at each attempt to nag, and used regularly for a few days, often succeeds in breaking the habit. Needless to say, these methods can only be used in training, and then only intermittently otherwise they lose their effect.

In some books you will find a suggestion that a stick fitted between the bits of the two leaders is the answer to nagging or one-sided horses. In theory it should work but in practice it causes more problems than it solves and in any case I think it is a dangerous device.

While wheelers may not be so inclined to nag, they can develop other aggravating habits such as leaning on each other or pulling away from each other. This can sometimes be cured by work in single harness to a very light vehicle. It may also be due to wrong coupling of the reins or fear of the pole, or loose pole straps which allow the pole to thrash about between the horses. It may be that the pole is the wrong length or the wrong height.

One-sided horses, that is, horses which persistently either carry their heads to one side or which turn more readily in one direction than the other, can also be very trying. Riding can help a lot but sometimes the occasional use of a small pad with short brush bristles on one side and fitted on the bar of the bit between the bit

(left) Balancing rein. *(Author's Collection)*

(right) Anti-nagging line attached to leader's bridle. *(Author's Collection)*

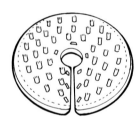

Bristle pad.

and the side of the mouth is frequently sufficiently irritating to encourage the horse to turn its head away from the bristles. A balancing or bearing rein can help in some cases but with the same limitations as apply to a nagging horse. However, it is worth remembering that if one horse works harder than its neighbour and the coupling reins have not been adjusted to compensate, then the more active horse is bound to feel its rein more than the coupling rein and thus have its head pulled outwards.

In fact, one of the most difficult problems is the adjustment of the coupling reins. It is fairly obvious that if you shorten both coupling reins equally, in other words by decreasing the number of holes in the reins nearest the hand, the effect will be to bring the horses' heads together. Letting them out will have the opposite effect, namely to pull the horses' heads apart.

A more complicated problem arises when one of the two horses, either in the wheel or in the lead, works harder and therefore goes ahead of the other, or when one has a longer neck. This problem, and the cure, is so well described by Fairman Rogers in his *Manual of Coaching* that I can do no better than to quote the relevant paragraphs in full:

Each draught-rein has attached to it a rein which passes to the bit of the other horse, so that a pull on the offside rein, for instance, will be communicated to the offside of each horse's mouth. It is obvious that to do this evenly, the inside, or coupling-rein must have a certain definite length from the bit to the point at which it is buckled to the draught-rein. Owing to its crossing over between the horses, the coupling-rein must be longer than that part of the draught-rein which is in front of the coupling-buckle, or else the horses' heads will be brought too near together. Usually, with horses of the same size, and at the proper distance apart, the coupling-rein will be four inches longer than the draught-rein for the leaders, and five or six inches longer for the wheelers; and, if the saddler has made the reins properly, the coupling-buckle will then be in the middle hole of the fifteen holes which are punched in the draught-rein. If the horses, when driven in this way, are found to be too far apart, the taking up of each coupling-rein one or two holes shorter on each draught-rein will bring them nearer together, supposing always that the horses are of the same size and that they hold their heads alike.

On driving them, however, it will be very likely found that one of the horses holds his head in, with his neck bent, and the other holds his head out and forward. The coupling-rein of the former will be, therefore, slack, and the horse being less restrained will go away from the pole until his inside rein becomes tight. To counteract this, it will be necessary to shorten, or take up his coupling, remembering always that his coupling is that which goes from his bit to the draught-rein of the other horse.

It may also happen that one horse is more eager or free than the other, and will be too far ahead; in which case the taking up of his coupling will bring him back — that is, it will draw more tightly on his bit and restrain him.

In both cases, however, the shortening of the coupling-rein will bring the horses' heads nearer together; and if their distance apart was originally correct and is to be maintained,

whatever is taken up in one coupling must be let out in the other.

This is shown in the diagram, where the relative distances are exaggerated to show the action more clearly.

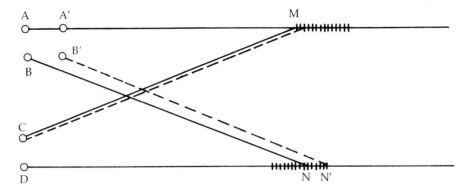

When the horses are working exactly alike, the reins are arranged as shown by the black lines; A and B are the two sides of the off horse's bit, C and D those of the near horse. The draught-reins AM and DN run straight to the coachman's hand. The coupling-reins are BN and CM, buckled to the draught-reins at N and M.

Now, if the off horse bends his neck so as to bring his head nearer to his body, both the reins which run to his bit will be too slack, and he will run forward and do more than his share of the work, while the near horse is held back. To prevent this, the off horse's coupling-rein BN is shortened by running it up the draught-rein to N', the last hole, until it comes just tight to the bit; but this obviously leaves the off draught-rein AM as slack as it was before, so that the coachman has to draw his hand back to bring it to bear upon the bit at A'. In so doing, however, he draws back the coupling-rein CM, and pulls the head of the near horse to the inside. To prevent this, the coupling-rein CM must be let out on its draught-rein exactly as much as the other coupling-rein has been taken up, which is equivalent to pulling back the draught-rein, whereupon the coupling-reins will have the positions shown by the dotted lines, with the buckle of C rein in the first hole, and all the reins will act evenly on both horses, notwithstanding that the mouth and bit of the off horse is nearer to the coachman's hand than that of the near horse.

If the horses are too far apart, but otherwise are working evenly, the coupling-reins must be shortened equally; or lengthened equally if they are too near together.

The fact that a horse, when he holds his head in, and curves his neck, is thereby practically lengthening his rein and consequently doing more than his share of the work, must be carefully remembered; simple as it appears, it is not always noticed by the coachman.

Reins are frequently made with three holes in the inside billet, or in both billets, the object being to prevent wear by changing the places where the bit touches them. These holes can be used to alter the length of the coupling-rein, and some coachmen seem to think that there is a difference between shortening it in this way and in moving the buckle up the draught-rein. A little reflection will show, however, that it is only a question of the distance between the part of the draught-rein where the coupling-rein is attached, and the bit, and that it is perfectly immaterial whether this distance is lengthened or shortened at one end or the other, of the coupling-rein. It is better to have only one hole in the billet; as a matter of fact it is rarely changed for the purpose of preventing wear, and if there is more than one hole and the billet is buckled in the wrong one, the coupling is thereby changed without the knowledge of the coachman. A renewal of the billets when they show the slightest sign of wear is the best precaution, and a most important one; nothing can be more dangerous than a damaged rein.

The conventional or 'English' way of holding the reins of a four-in-hand is to pass the near leader rein over the index finger of the left hand, the off leader rein goes directly under the same finger, the near wheeler rein goes under the off leader rein and the off wheeler rein goes under the middle finger. For all general purposes this is a very convenient method. The left hand and arm acts as the accelerator and brake by varying the pressure on the reins while the right hand is free to steer by pulling individual reins and to hold the whip. The problem is that it is very difficult to prevent the reins slipping through the fingers and this is particularly liable to happen to the near wheeler rein and it is not easy to re-adjust the reins quickly without looking down. If they get wet it becomes virtually impossible to hold the reins at all.

For the purpose of driving a coach down a road the 'English' method works very well, largely because sharp turns are only required at fairly long intervals so that there is plenty of time to adjust the reins and to pull the leaders out of draft by shortening their reins well before reaching the corner. In dressage the corners come thick and fast and there is no time to make any re-adjustments to the reins. In order to drive a test accurately it is absolutely vital to make sure that each rein is held precisely at the right length throughout the test. To achieve this you can mark the reins in some way or fit some sort of clamp on the reins or, better still, you can punch holes in the reins at the appropriate places and pass all four reins through a buckle or use some other device to hold them together. Then, whatever you do and whatever drama occurs or however hard it rains you can always be certain that with the buckle in the palm of your hand the reins cannot slip or get tangled.

It is probably a good idea to punch at least three holes in each rein two or three inches apart so that adjustments can be made for individual horses. The holes in the leaders' reins should be placed in such a way that when the buckle is put on the middle hole of all the reins, the leaders are just out of draft when the wheelers are just feeling their bits.

The problem of controlling four horses in the hazards and while driving the cones becomes much more acute. Many good drivers have demonstrated that it can be done with the conventional 'English' method but it is, without doubt, much more easily done by driving 'two-

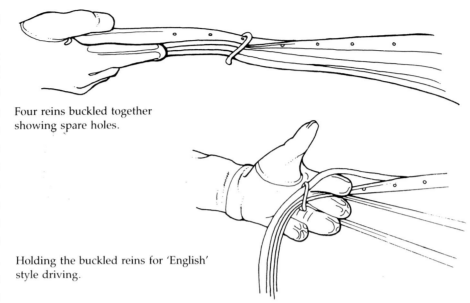

Four reins buckled together showing spare holes.

Holding the buckled reins for 'English' style driving.

handed'. It may look a bit agricultural, but it works. In fact the Hungarians use such a method all the time. There are various ways of doing it. In principle it means holding the near leader and near wheeler reins in the left hand and the off leader and off wheeler reins in the right hand. As luck would have it, the holes you have punched in the reins for the dressage happen to come in very handy for two-handed driving. All that needs to be done is to pass the two near reins through one small buckle and the two off reins through another and to hold the buckles in the palms of the hands with the leader reins passing over the index fingers and the wheeler reins under the little fingers.

It will be immediately evident that if you pull with the left hand and ease with the right, all four horses will turn to the left together. However, if you pull with the left hand and roll your

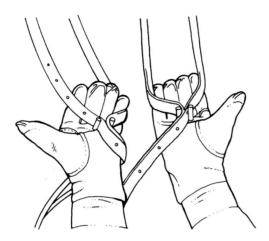

Buckled reins for two-handed driving.

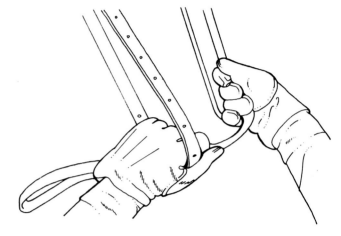

Wrists 'rolled' for a turn to the left. The near leader and the off wheeler reins are shortened to turn the leaders and 'hold off' the wheelers.

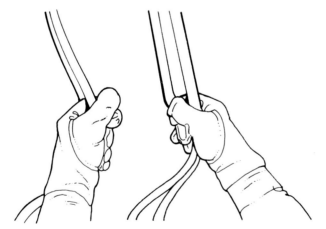

For two-handed driving the buckles are in the palms of the hands and act as a 'datum' point.

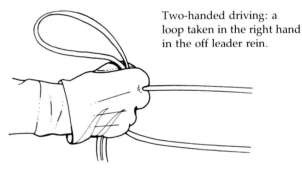

Two-handed driving: a loop taken in the right hand in the off leader rein.

Two-handed driving: a loop taken in the left hand in the near leader rein.

left wrist towards you while easing with your right hand, and roll your right wrist away from you, the leaders will turn before the wheelers. In order to turn a sharp corner to the left, all that needs to be done is to stretch forward and take up a loop in the near wheeler rein, holding it between the index and middle fingers. Nothing will happen until you bring your left hand back to its normal position whereupon the leaders will turn to the left while the right hand holds the wheelers out of the corner. Once the leaders are round, the loop is slipped and the left hand pulls the wheelers round. With practice the horses can be driven extremely accurately by this method.

There is, of course, one important potential risk about buckling the reins together. If by some mischance the leaders break away, you will be pulled off the box, although this has happened to me while holding the reins 'English' fashion in my left hand without a buckle.

The most difficult problem is a horse that pulls. The obvious answer is to use a more severe bit but it may not always be the right answer. A severe bit tends to deaden the mouth so that a still more severe bit has to be used until the ironmongery becomes so complicated and unpleasant that the Steward charged with inspecting bits would have a fit. Therefore it is well worth experimenting with a variety of bits of different shapes and materials. It can happen that you suddenly stumble on something that does the trick. If nothing seems to work the only answer is to get rid of the horse. There is nothing more dangerous than trying to drive hazards with a leader that pulls, while a pulling wheeler throws the whole team off balance.

CHAPTER 4

HARNESS

Broadly speaking the choice of harness lies between what is generally called 'English' or neck collar and 'Hungarian' or breast collar harness. The difference is that in 'English' harness the horses wear collars around their necks to which the traces are attached, whereas in 'Hungarian' harness the traces are attached to a broad strap which lies across their chests. The relative advantages are that the 'English' collar harness is more efficient in that the horses can exert a greater pull, although this is not a vital factor for big horses as the four-in-hand competition carriages are relatively light. The 'Hungarian' harness, by contrast, is about half the weight. The 'English' collars need to be individually fitted to each horse otherwise there is a serious risk of rubbing and sore shoulders. The 'Hungarian' harness, on the other hand, is constructed with a number of straps and buckles which make it possible to adjust to a fairly wide range of horse shapes, but a more limited range of horse sizes. As the breast collar is loose-fitting there is also a greater tendency for the shoulders to be rubbed until the horse gets used to it. One great advantage of this strap construction is that the harness is easier to repair and if anything breaks it can usually be replaced temporarily by a piece of string or a spare halter.

There is one absolutely vital point about 'Hungarian' harness. The wheeler traces must on no account be attached to the roller-bolts fixed to the splinter bar. The carriage must be fitted with two centrally pivoted (or swingle) bars mounted on the splinter bar with vertical or horizontal roller-bolts at each end.

The reason is that the horse's shoulders have to work inside the breast collar and if the traces are fixed rigidly to the splinter bar so that there is no movement in the collar, the shoulders rub against it. If you watch breast collar traces attached to a pivoting bar you will see that the bar moves to and fro with every pace taken by the horse.

Swingle bars are not so necessary with the 'English' collar harness because the collar goes round the neck which remains relatively motion-

(left) Horses in 'English' harness. (Author's Collection)

(right) Horses in 'Hungarian' harness. (Author's Collection)

Swingle bars. (Alf. Baker)

Trace carriers and breeching. *(Author's Collection)*

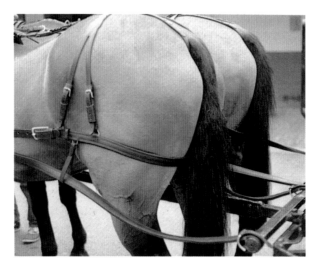

less while the moving shoulders do not come directly in contact with the collar. However, there is much to be said for using swingle bars even in 'English' harness.

While an 'English' collar needs to be individually fitted to each horse, it is equally important to adjust the breast collar so that it lies in the right position. In principle it must not be so high that it presses on the wind pipe nor so low that it catches against the front legs as they swing forward. The wheelers' breast collars are held in place by a neck strap and the pole strap and, if necessary, by a strap from the girth to the collar. The leaders' collars only need to be held up by a neck strap.

It is always worth fitting trace carriers to both wheelers and leaders, as without them there is a greater chance that a horse will get a leg over a trace. It may be a minor matter but a leg over a trace may well start a horse kicking which can end up with a great deal of damage. Some horses don't mind a trace between their legs but if you leave it there for any time it will inevitably rub the horse badly.

While on the subject of traces, there is nothing more irritating than for a trace to become disconnected for some reason or other. Spring clips on the leaders' traces may look secure enough but they have a nasty habit of coming off at critical moments. Furthermore they have sharp points and if anything goes wrong they can cause injury. In practice the system whereby the trace is pushed through a metal link at the end to form a loop, known as a 'running loop', which is then slipped over the end of the bar, or roller-bolt, is the most satisfactory. As soon as any weight comes on the trace it pulls the loop tight and a little leather tongue attached to the

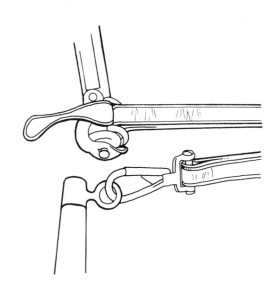

'Running loop' *(top)*, and 'spring clip' *(below)*.

bar and slipped over the trace and secured to a small knob on the end of the bar keeps the trace from falling off, although I have never known a running loop trace come off.

By far the best solution is to use a quick release device, such as that described by yachtsmen as a 'snap-shackle'. These can be fitted to the swingle bars to take the ends of the wheelers' and leaders' traces. The same device can be used to connect the pole straps to the collars of the wheelers and a similar device can also be used to attach the connecting strap between the leaders. These 'snap-shackles' can be released even when under tension, so that in an emergency the horses can be disconnected from the carriage without having to cut any of the harness. They also make it much easier in putting-to and disconnecting a team in the ordinary course of events. You only have to release eleven snap-shackles (eight traces, two pole straps and the connecting strap between the leaders) and the horses are free.

For competition work I find that it is best to bring the wheeler horses as close to the carriage as possible, making sure that they cannot touch the wheels or the springs with any part of their hind legs as they stretch back at an extended trot. The leaders, on the other hand, are best given rather longer traces than normally necessary. The point is that they will be required to 'fold back' very sharply in some obstacles and the longer traces give them a better chance to keep clear of the wheelers without putting any pull on the pole end.

Another way of giving the leaders more flexi-bility is to fit a hinged link, about eight to ten inches long, at the end of the pole and attach the swingle trees to that. This allows the leaders to turn quite sharply before pulling the end of the pole across.

In dressage tests the wheelers are required to push the carriage backwards and it is more than likely that they will have to do it, sooner or later,

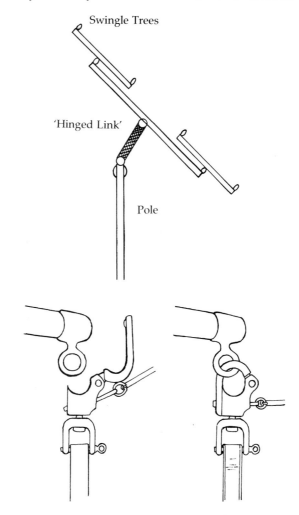

Hinged link on end of pole (*top*), and 'snap shackle' quick release device (*below*).

HRH The Duke of Edinburgh's team of Fell ponies in webbing harness. (*Alf. Baker*)

in a hazard. Furthermore, even though carriages are fitted with brakes, the wheelers will also be expected to hold the carriage back when going down steep hills. They can do all this by simply leaning back on the pole straps but it makes matters much easier and gives the wheelers more confidence and control if they are fitted with breeching. However, as with all items of harness it must be fitted just right.

In my experience most accidents are caused by something breaking. It is therefore extremely important to make sure that every item of harness is sound and in good condition. It goes without saying that the complete harness needs to be very carefully adjusted to each individual horse so that it fits exactly and every part is capable of performing its particular function. This means that the harness should be carefully inspected each time before moving off.

Conventional harness is made of leather but several variations of webbing harness are appearing on the market. Nylon webbing without leather or felt covering seems to rub badly but cotton or polyester webbing seems to be softer. A great advantage of webbing harness is that it can be washed in a washing machine and dried in a spin drier, unlike leather which needs a great deal of laborious cleaning and attention.

CHAPTER 5

CARRIAGES

—————•—————

A full FEI driving competition requires that a carriage should be as smart as possible for the dressage competition; as short and narrow as possible, with a low centre of gravity, easy for the grooms to get on and off, and weighing at least 600 kg (300 kg for ponies), for the marathon competition; and with the shortest wheelbase, and widest permissible track width for the obstacles driving competition. To find a vehicle that incorporates all these conflicting features is quite a problem.

There has been a great deal of discussion about the idea of a dual (or triple) purpose vehicle and, as a matter of fact, I drove such a carriage in two European and one World Championship and Sir John Miller drove it in all tests at the 1980 World Championships. In each case the turnout was placed within the first three in presentation and, in spite of being turned over in Hungary in 1978, it completed the course and I drove it in the obstacles driving competition on the last day. So a dual purpose carriage is possible. The only practical disadvan-tage is that some sort of carriage is needed for exercise and practice right up to the start of the competition and, if only one is available, it means that a great deal of cleaning, polishing and touching up has to take place at the last moment, which is naturally not very popular with the grooms or with the driver as he can't have it when he wants it.

Apart from that it is not easy to design an ideal marathon carriage which has either the looks or the features necessary for the other competitions. However, it can be done and I will describe an attempt to solve this problem further on.

I have indicated some of the features required by competition carriages. There are also a number of limitations and constraints that need to be taken into account in the design of such carriages.

The height and length of a carriage is dictated by the radius of its wheels and by the track width of (i.e. distance between) the front wheels. The greater the diameter of the wheels, the higher

Dual purpose carriage (see also page 52). (*Author's Collection*)

the axles are from the ground and the further apart the axles need to be and hence the longer the wheelbase.

There are two other features about the wheels. The suspension of any vehicle is improved by the reduction in 'unsprung' weight. For example, in two carriages of the same weight, where the body of one is very light and suspended on springs over proportionally heavy wheels, axles and brakes (the unsprung weight), any jolt to the wheels will be communicated directly to the body because there is not sufficient inertia in the light body to activate the springs. In the other case, where the unsprung weight (wheels, axles, brakes) is very light, the jolt will force the wheels to react but the proportionally heavy weight of the body will cause the springs to compress and therefore cushion the body from the jolt. This is quite important because an unexpected unsprung jolt can easily throw a driver off the box seat.

The suspension and the ease of running of a carriage is also influenced by the diameter of the wheels. Imagine a small wheel of, say, a foot in diameter approaching a brick lying in its path. The angle at which the radius of the wheel hits the brick is relatively steep so that the wheel is suddenly forced to jump up over the brick. Now imagine a wheel of, say, 4 feet in diameter approaching the same brick. The angle at which the radius hits the brick is much flatter allowing the wheel to climb gradually over the brick, providing a smoother ride. It is also quite apparent that, from the horse's point of view, it is easier to drag a carriage with big diameter

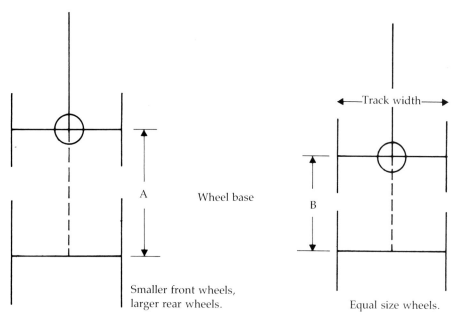

Smaller front wheels, larger rear wheels.

Equal size wheels.

wheels, which ride more smoothly over rough going, than one with little wheels. Needless to say whatever size of wheels is chosen they will definitely run better if they are mounted on tapered roller bearings at the ends of the axles. The important point is that the roller bearings should be big and strong enough for the weight of the carriage and the going likely to be encountered.

One of the very obvious features about the traditional design of carriages is that the front wheels are invariably of a smaller diameter than the back wheels. The reason for this, apart from big back wheels providing a better ride, is that in order to turn a carriage, the whole front axle pivots about its centre under the turn-table and one wheel (and at extreme angles, part of the splinter bar plus roller bolts) has to be able to swivel under the carriage. Small wheels are obviously more easily accommodated than big ones. In any case the height of the box seat is virtually dictated by the height of the turn-table above the ground and the height of the turn-table is itself dictated by the diameter of the front wheels, and front wheels equal in size to the normal back wheels would put the box seat much too high.

Again, going on the principle that most accidents occur when things break, I firmly believe that competition carriages should be as strong as reasonably possible, within the overall weight limitation. There is really little point in designing a carriage and then having to add weights to it to reach the legal minimum when the extra weight could be used to make the carriage that

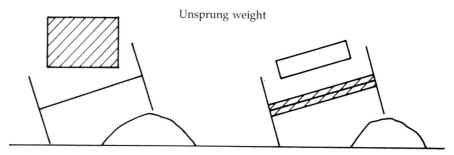

Unsprung weight

Heavy carriage, low unsprung weight.   Light carriage, high unsprung weight.

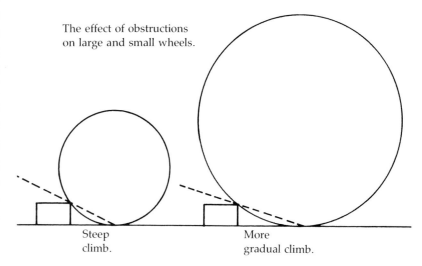

The effect of obstructions on large and small wheels.

Steep climb.

More gradual climb.

much more unbreakable. Although wooden wheels strong enough for normal use are lighter and can safely be used in pony carriages, in horse carriages, unless they are very heavily built, they are liable to break in rough going with very unpleasant results. Therefore light metal alloy wheels are preferable.

Traditional carriages are sprung for normal road work and for that purpose their suspension

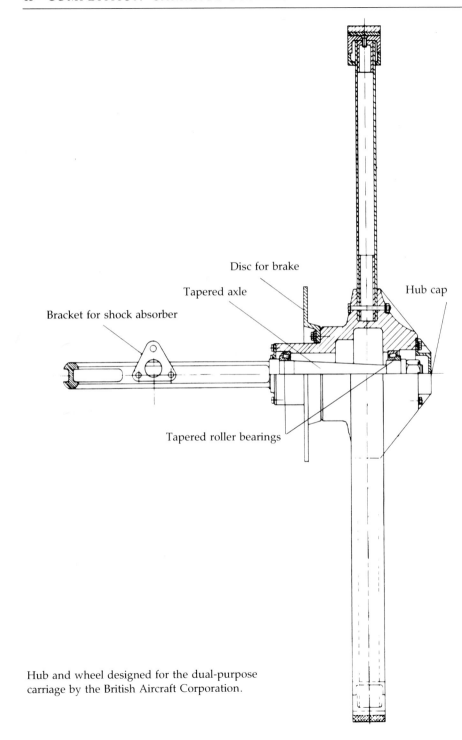

Disc for brake

Tapered axle

Bracket for shock absorber

Hub cap

Tapered roller bearings

Hub and wheel designed for the dual-purpose carriage by the British Aircraft Corporation.

provides a very good ride, but their springs are relatively soft. The result is that if the carriage is taken over rough ground the body leaps up and down like a yo-yo. You can get over this in a new carriage by making the springs much stiffer but then you get a much rougher ride. The solution has been kindly invented by the motor manufacturers in the shape of shock absorbers. These, combined with proper weight distribution and the right amount of springing, produce a reasonably smooth ride over most going.

The rather soft springs in traditional carriages, together with the fairly slack construction of the turn-table assembly and the bendiness of wooden poles meant that the carriage end of the pole could be rigidly fixed between the splinter bar and the lower part of the turn-table. In spite of this rigid attachment the pole was able to move up and down with reasonable flexibility yet without thrashing up and down and hitting the wheelers in the teeth when the going was rough. Early carriages used 'C' springs and leather straps. A later development was the 'leaf spring'. Best carriages are usually fitted with these and they are still to be seen on railway carriages and many heavy goods vehicles. Many cross-country carriages are now fitted with a 'trailing-link' suspension system. The advantage of this system is that it provides four-wheel independent suspension and, owing to its very simple design, it is less likely to break.

In an all-metal carriage, with stiff springs and a more or less rigid turn-table, the pole cannot be attached in the same way as every movement of the front wheels would be communicated to

the pole and in uneven going the pole end would either be pulling the wheelers down by their necks or lifting them off their feet.

In order to overcome this problem a metal pole on a metal carriage needs to be pivoted vertically about the pin holding it in place in the bracket attached to the splinter bar. This bracket can have two pairs of holes so that the pole can be cocked up to compensate for the weight of the swingle-trees when driving a team; and lowered when used for a pair. The pole needs to be held in the right position by a spring above the heel end of the pole, and prevented from thrashing up by a damper spring underneath the heel. A number of systems for controlling the essential movement of the pole have been

devised in recent years, including leaf springs, coil springs, a combination of spring and damper, and a trailing-link type suspension.

In a traditional carriage the wooden pole and swingle-trees, being relatively light, did not exert much pressure on the turn-table. In a metal carriage with heavier pole and swingle-trees and a more rigid turn-table, the friction between the upper and lower parts of the turn-table is greater. Therefore either a bigger diameter turn-table is required, or a separate arc fitted behind the top half of the turn-table on which a slide or roller can run will help to take some of the weight and allow it to rotate more easily. If the upper − or lower − part of the turn-table is fitted with two or three rollers at

(above left) Shock absorber fitted to the rear axle of the dressage carriage. *(Alf. Baker)*

(above right) Turn-table. *(Alf. Baker)*

the circumference, the friction is much reduced.

One of the great difficulties in negotiating hazards is that the pole and turn-table are rigidly attached to each other. This means that as soon as the wheelers move the pole to one side, the carriage immediately follows. Unless the driver ensures that there is room for the front wheels to get past a gatepost, for instance, the inside front wheel is very likely to hit, and probably get stuck behind, the gatepost. During the late 1980s a new device appeared from the continent, which has become known as the 'bendy pole'. It is a misnomer, as the pole does not bend, but it allows the carriage to 'bend' round a gatepost by arranging for the sideways movement of the pole to be delayed before it is conveyed to the turn-table. One very important point about fitting this system is that it requires the inside wheeler to move ahead of the outside wheeler and, unless something is done about it, the outside trace on the outside wheeler will either break or prevent the horses from turning. The cure is to fit a swivelling cross-bar at the end of the pole to which the pole straps are attached. The movement of the bar allows the inside wheeler to move ahead and the outside wheeler to drop back in the turns.

The easiest way to understand the system is to study the illustration on page 43. The system undoubtedly works in the hazards, but it has one unpleasant drawback. For some reason, which for the moment has not been satisfactorily explained, a carriage travelling fast downhill on a slippery surface (wet grass or gravel) tends to snake from side to side. The back end of the carriage flaps to and fro like the end of a flag in a high wind. This can be very unnerving and I remember the first time I witnessed this phenomenon. I went up to see the last part of Section C at the 1990 Drumlanrig Event and I got there just in time to watch George Bowman coming down the hill at his usual pace. I then noticed that his carriage was behaving very oddly and the expression on the face of his groom made it abundantly clear that all was not at all well. Everything seemed to be normal in front, but the back end was waving to and fro in a most alarming fashion. Various explanations have been put forward, but the problem has yet to be completely solved. Meanwhile a variety of designs have been tried out but several failed to stand up to the rigours of Section E, with unfortunate consequences.

The rules say that no part of a carriage may be wider than the wheels, other than the splinter bar. (Hubs that stick out are, anyway, extremely undesirable for obvious reasons, although some continental drivers have got over the problem by fitting 'hub-fenders' between the hub and the rim of the wheel – but it looks unsightly.) The width of the splinter bar or the swingle bars is effectively dictated by the width of the horses. If the bars are too narrow all that happens is that the outside traces rub the wheeler's hind legs raw. As far as obstacle driving is concerned, the rules require all carriages in each class to have a standard track width. This is so that, during the competition, the width of the cones does not have to be changed for individual carriages in the class.

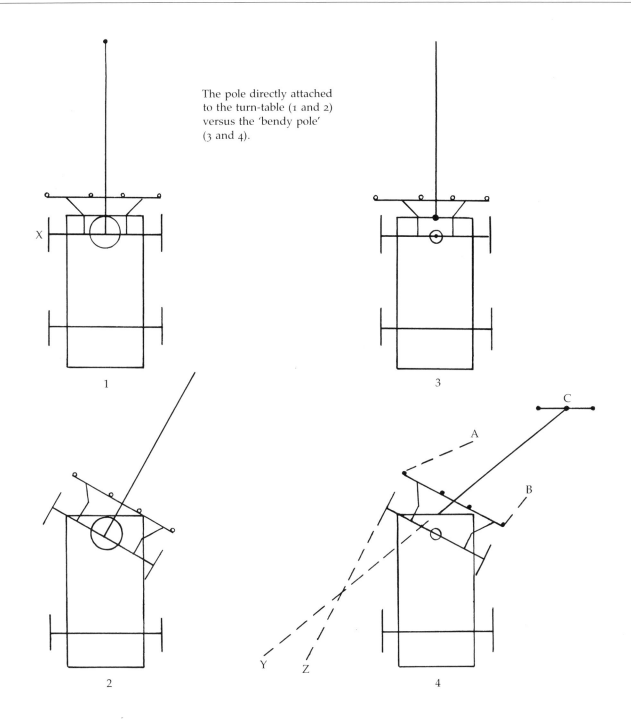

The pole directly attached
to the turn-table (1 and 2)
versus the 'bendy pole'
(3 and 4).

The actual shape and dimensions of the box seat and foot board are a matter for personal choice but there are certain factors that are worth considering. One problem is that anxiety and concentration seem to encourage drivers to lean forward. If the box seat is fairly flat it tends to produce what has been described as 'the loo position' which does not impress the judges. Therefore for dressage and obstacles the seat can well be sloped forward so as to put more weight on the legs which helps the driver to sit upright, and incidentally, it also gives greater power to hold the horses if the need arises.

On the marathon, driving style is not as important as security, therefore a flatter, softer seat and contact with the back rest is preferable as it gives the driver a more secure base.

While on the subject of box seats, I find it very convenient to have a small drawer or locker fitted at the back and directly under the seat. It provides an accessible stowage for spare gloves, keys, stop-watches, odd buckles and other vital odds and ends. However, it does need clearing out every now and then as it tends to accumulate non-essential items, such as half a packet of Polo mints, elastic bands, the programme for the last competition, and postcards from Aunt Maud.

At one time, poles, splinter bars, bars and swingle-trees were all made of wood, but the risk of breakage is simply not worth it. I have had two broken poles (one metal, but it got fatigue) and I broke three wooden swingle-tree bars in the 1976 European Championships in Holland and I would rather not repeat the experience. Although they are heavier, all these parts can be made of the appropriate metal and with careful design the swingle-trees can be made neater, more compact and a good deal less noisy.

The drawback to a metal pole is that it can be narrower than a wooden pole and therefore even less pleasant for the wheelers when they bump into it. It is therefore a good idea to wrap the pole for most of its length with a foam rubber material and bind it on with broad harness tape (making sure that the foam is completely covered by the tape otherwise water will get in).

Swingle-trees for the leaders and swingle bars for the wheelers can be made of scaffold tube with aluminium plugs set in each end flanged on the outer ends to keep the trace loops from

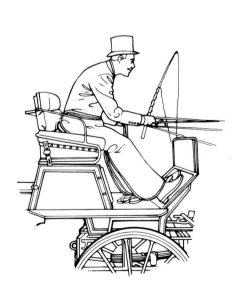

The 'loo' position.

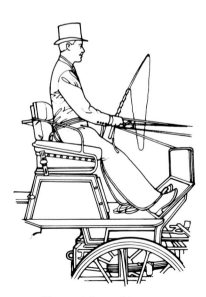

The upright position.

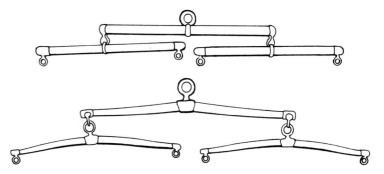

(above left) Inclined seat gives a better leg position for the driver (see diagram of upright position, page 44). *(Alf. Baker)*

(above right) Lockers under the seats of the 'best' carriage. *(Alf. Baker)*

(left) The pole wrapped with foam rubber and bound on with harness tape. *(Alf. Baker)*

Compact metal swingle-trees *(top)* fitted for 'quick-release clips' (snap-shackles) compared to traditional wooden swingle-trees fitted for 'spring clips'.

Disc brakes. *(Alf. Baker)*

slipping off. A good finish for these bars is to have them covered with black plastic: it is not easily scratched, the wheelers cannot bite it and there is no clanging of metal.

Foot brakes are highly desirable and there is a choice between the traditional carriage brakes, which act on the tyres, and shoe brakes or disc brakes which are fitted to the rear axle. The traditional type of brakes works reasonably well on metal tyres but their effect varies rather too drastically on rubber tyres, particularly when they are wet, and they are noisy. The drawback

about shoe brakes is that they take some time to recover their action after going through water. The criticism of disc brakes is that they are too harsh, but this is only true if fitted to traditionally built carriages. Even so, it should be possible to adjust them so that they can be applied progressively and without harm to the carriage.

Whether the rules require them or not, it is a good practice for competition carriages to be fitted with hand brakes. Traditional hand brakes work on a ratchet device which holds the brake lever in the 'on' position. Shoe and disc brakes operated by a foot pedal only require a small ratchet device fitted to the foot pedal lever which can be pulled into position rather like a motor car choke lever. Press the foot pedal down, pull the lever out and the ratchet holds the brakes on. Press the pedal again and the lever can be pushed in and the brakes released. Even better is to fit a hand operated valve in the hydraulic system which can be closed when the brakes are 'on' thus keeping the pressure in the system. Switch off and the pressure is released.

If you put all these factors together, the ideal solution to the carriage problem seems to be one smart traditional-looking carriage for dressage and the obstacle driving with a fairly high box seat — for good visibility — and a forward facing back seat for the grooms.

As no minimum weight is specified for carriages used in dressage and obstacles tests the materials used and the method of construction is a matter for personal choice.

A second purpose-designed carriage is then required for practice, exercise and the marathon.

(above) Traditional looking 'best' horse carriage for the dressage and obstacle (cones) competitions. Light alloy wheels and metal pole. Made by Artistic Iron Products, Newark. *(Alf. Baker)*

Best pony carriage. *(Alf. Baker)*

Horse team cross-country (marathon) carriage. Short and narrow with an open 'chariot' type back. *(Alf. Baker)*

It should have a metal frame, light alloy wheels, metal splinter bar, swingle bars, swingle-trees and pole. Four equal size wheels of about 3 feet (1 metre) diameter (for horses) allows the box seat to be at a reasonable height, while keeping the back part of the carriage and therefore the centre of gravity as low as possible. Equal size wheels also have the advantage that only one spare is required.

There is no need for a back seat for the grooms — they seem to prefer to stand throughout the marathon anyway — so that the back can be left open rather like a chariot. In order to make it easier to get in and out and to reduce the centre of gravity the back platform can be fitted between the back springs and just above the back axle. The back platform can be lowered even further by attaching the back spring above rather than below the back axle. Lockers under the box seat and at the front end of the back platform should provide sufficient stowage for the obligatory spares, tools and other bits of equipment.

The three vulnerable places on a marathon carriage, when negotiating hazards, are the front wheels, the outer ends of the splinter bar or the outer ends of the swingle bars, and the gap between the front and back wheels. There is not much you can do about a splinter bar with fixed upright roller-bolts. Such a bar has to be at right angles to the pole which means that if the horses come round a tree or a post a bit too quickly either the front wheel or the splinter bar is liable to come up all standing against it and you will probably lose one or two traces.

With swingle bars fixed to the splinter bar it is possible to angle the outer portions of the splinter bar (outside the pivot point of the swingle bar) backwards so that it does not hit an obstruction square on. But this leaves the

(left) Back platform of horse team cross-country (marathon) carriage, including lockers and back axle. *(Alf. Baker)*

(right) Drawers under driving seat of horse team marathon carriage *(Alf. Baker)*

(above) Swingle bars of horse team marathon carriage with spring clips attached.

(above right) Mudguard of horse team marathon carriage (Alf. Baker)

swingle bars, to which the traces are attached, to take the full brunt of the contact. However, if the swingle bar is allowed to swing past the angled splinter bar it will transfer the contact from the pivoting bar and trace to the angled end of the splinter bar. The travel of the swingle bar can be limited by fitting a stop at the appropriate place, then if a trace should be broken, the swingle bar comes up against the stop and cannot move any further forward and therefore the horse can still help to pull the carriage at least clear of the exit gate. It is also important to limit the movement of the inner end of the swingle bar so as to give the inside wheeler the ability to pull on his outside trace.

In order to prevent obstructions getting between the front and back wheels a 'mud guard' above the wheels starting above the middle of the front wheels and running back just inside the outer rim of the wheels to a point above the middle of the back wheel seems to meet the case.

If the horizontal space between this bumper bar and the carriage body is filled in it helps to make it look like a mud guard and it also provides a useful platform for the grooms when they lean out on slopes and tight corners. Oddly enough these 'wings' are not as noticeable as you might expect.

However, a serious problem can occur if the

front wheel comes up against an obstruction below the level of the splinter bar 'fender', such as the end of a log lying on the ground. Short of lifting the front wheels off the ground and moving the front part of the carriage sideways, almost impossible to do in practice, the wheelers have got to push the carriage backwards until the wheel is clear and then the pole end must be pulled round so that the wheel clears the obstruction as the wheelers move forward. As such a situation can easily bend the pole away from the trapped wheel it makes the problem that much more difficult. As a matter of fact, hazards which include obstructions such as logs and trees with pronounced root branches can be very dangerous. Horses trip and clamber over the logs, the drivers can't see them clearly and a front wheel can easily get lodged between the root branches or up against the flat end of a log. Furthermore, if the carriage runs up the root it can easily turn over.

As the grooms spend most of the time standing up it is a good idea to provide hand rails wherever possible.

One solution to the problem of making a dual purpose carriage is to start with a conventional metal under-carriage with larger back wheels and smaller front wheels in light alloy. The diameter of the wheels depends on the size of the horses or ponies to be driven. On the upper body, the box seat and footboard are of normal comfortable dimensions but the rear portion is so constructed that the complete back seat with the locker and floor board attached can be lifted off. This leaves an open 'chariot' type back

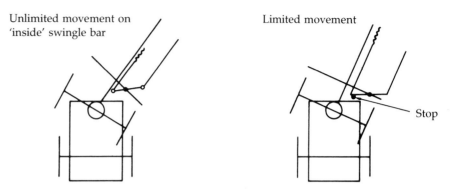

The stop on the inside of the splinter bar ensures that if a wheeler loses an inside trace it continues to pull on the outside trace without too much change in its position.

section and all that is needed is a portable back floor board fitted in place over the back axle as low as possible between the upper part of the springs. In practice the level of the floor board will be dictated by the position of the shock absorbers.

An extra refinement is to fit removable side panels so as to protect them from getting dirty on exercise and from the rigours of the marathon.

As the carriage is to be used for all competitions the axle joining the front wheels can be cut in half and the two parts slid into a box section bar fixed in place of the normal axle, and the stub axles bolted into position inside it. (The bolts go down through holes in the box section and through holes in the solid axles inside them.) In this way the optimum track width for the marathon can be selected for both front and back wheels. As all carriages in the same class need to have the same track width for the obstacle driving, all that needs to be done is to take the bolts out of the front axle and

Dual purpose pony carriage adjusted for marathon (see also page 38). (*Author's Collection*)

pull the solid parts out of the box section, and then slip the bolts back through the same holes in the box section and a second pair of holes in the solid parts of the axle.

To reconvert the carriage for the marathon the back seat is lifted off, the side panels removed, the rear undercarriage moved forward, the front wheels pushed in, the lamp brackets removed, and the removable floor board put back in place.

An altogether different approach to the design of a marathon carriage is an adaptation of the 'equi-rotal' system which was invented in the last century. In principle the front wheels, splinter bar, pole and box seat are all fixed together (as in a 'curricle'). The back wheels together with the rear over-carriage are then attached to the front body by a hinge or a turn-table. The effect is that the back wheels are 'towed' around behind the front wheels, the carriage bending in the middle, as it were. The guns and limbers of the King's Troop RHA operate on this system. There is no difference as far as the horses are concerned as they continue to pull an articulated vehicle, but the driver now finds himself driving the wheelers as if he were driving a single horse because his seat moves with the pole.

This type of carriage is less likely to get stuck once the front wheels are past an obstruction although a conventional carriage with 'wings' is equally safe, provided the obstruction is not lower than the 'wings' or the step fender in front of the back wheels. Both types of carriage are equally vulnerable to an obstruction catching a front wheel. The equi-rotal type is probably less likely to turn over in a corner as the back end acts as a 'counter-weight' on the inside of the turn.

In the early years of the driving competition, there was one particular issue that excited the members of the FEI Driving Committee. They were under pressure from what might be termed the 'reactionaries' to prevent the use of new-fangled designs and unconventional materials in the construction of carriages. The 'progressives' on the other hand maintained that it was better to let these things be tried in case they turned out to be safer or more appropriate. I am glad to say that the latter won and I believe that all driving has become much safer as a result.

After the horses and harness the most important piece of equipment for a driving competition is the carriage and, like any mechanical assembly, it needs regular maintenance and a particularly thorough check before a competition. There is such a thing as the perversity of inanimate objects, and that, coupled with Murphy's Law which states that if anything can go wrong – it will, means that a carriage which has performed perfectly for months will elect the morning of the competition to develop some mechanical psychiatric problem. I write from bitter experience as after months of perfect operation my brakes seized up after a mile on Section A at the World Championships at Windsor in 1980. Be warned.

CHAPTER 6

THE DRIVER

I am going to assume that anyone intending to enter for a four-in-hand FEI driving competition is reasonably competent in the basic techniques of four-in-hand driving. The object of this short chapter is to give what I hope will be some useful hints to drivers who are sufficiently ambitious to enter a driving competition.

As you are going to spend quite long periods on the box seat it is a good idea to make sure that you are comfortable. As I have already mentioned, a flat-topped seat and bent legs are not conducive to an elegant position on the box. The art is to get the weight of the body evenly shared between the legs and the backside in such a way that the pull on the reins can be taken by the legs while keeping the upper part of the body upright. Any rowing coach will tell you that the power of the stroke depends on the push exerted by the legs. The position of the hands and arms will depend on how much the horses are pulling but if all is going well the elbows can be kept close to the body with the hands just above the lap.

While everyone else on a carriage has hands free to allow them to hold on to something, the driver can only hold on to the reins and, as any rail built up around his hips, other than a back rest, is bound to interfere with his elbows or with the butt end of the whip, he is always in danger of being thrown off the box. With any luck this is unlikely to happen in the dressage or obstacles, but it is a real hazard on the marathon — it has happened to me twice and others have had the same experience. A sensible precaution is to wear a loose-fitting belt outside all clothing so that a considerate groom can grab hold of it in moments of anxiety, and when you feel him grabbing you know he is anxious, even if you don't know why.

The appropriate dress for dressage and obstacles depends on the style of turnout, but, in principle, if you are driving a team of horses in a turnout with 'English' harness, either a grey or a black top hat is expected. If it is a team of Mountain or Moorland ponies, a bowler or straw hat and a tweed jacket is acceptable. If you look at pictures or photographs of people wearing top hats you will notice that they only look elegant when they are placed upright on the head, that is, not leaning backwards. In order to wear them upright they need to be placed fairly well forward on the forehead. The same applies to bowler hats.

As any clothes below the waist are hidden by the apron, a short dark jacket is quite adequate but, of course, a tail coat looks better off the box. The only thing against tail coats is that it is not easy to avoid sitting on the tails. However, the most important point about any jacket is that there must be plenty of room around the

The driver concentrates on the hazard while the groom holds on to the loose fitting belt around his waist.
(Findlay Davidson)

shoulders, otherwise the sleeves ride up the arms, the back rides up the neck and all sensation is liable to be cut off from the arms by the tightness at the shoulders. A lightweight overcoat worn instead of a jacket can be very comfortable.

As far as I can make out aprons or knee rugs are designed to keep the ends of the reins from rubbing saddle soap on to your trousers. They are obligatory, but their material, colour and design can be according to taste, within reason. Some drivers prefer them to cover their legs right down to their feet, others are content with 'mini' aprons but these should at least reach the knees. Most aprons are held on by leather straps and buckles but I find that 'Velcro' instead of a buckle is more convenient.

Aprons used to be obligatory for the marathon but if they are used they are best kept small so that they don't get in the way in an emergency. It is quite a good idea to have them made of some washable material such as moleskin or linen.

In wet weather it is worth remembering that if you just wear a short rainproof jacket the water tends to run down and collect on the seat. Therefore either a long raincoat (not convenient for the marathon), or a short jacket and waterproof trousers, is most practical. It is also worth bearing in mind that some waterproof trousers tie at the waist and have a slit up the front. If the jacket does not cover the slit, you may be in for an interesting experience when the rain water runs down the jacket and into the slit.

There are no rules about dress for the marathon but there is no doubt that some degree of uniformity between the driver and grooms makes a better impression. Grooms are well advised to wear gym shoes so that they can run faster in moments of crisis and if they have to get down at a water crossing it doesn't matter if they get their shoes wet.

Gloves are a matter for personal comfort but for long periods of driving it is best to use fairly loose-fitting rough leather gloves. For the dressage, obstacles and the hazards it is quite a good idea to have more closely fitting and thinner gloves, buttoned at the wrist, as they make it easier to manipulate the reins.

The traditional type of glove for wet weather is made of 'string' or wool and these can cope fairly well with wet reins until they become sodden and then the reins begin to slip. A better way to prevent the reins slipping is to use a device for clamping the reins together so that the clamp lies in the palm. An even more certain way is to punch holes through the reins at the appropriate places and fit a buckle or buckles, as already described. The reins can then be held in the left hand in the normal way with the buckle resting in the palm or in both hands. This does not solve the glove problem in heavy rain but a buckle together with an ordinary pair of rubber domestic washing-up gloves provides as good a solution as any.

A driver has only two 'aids', the voice and the whip. The whip is both an aid and a handicap. It is an aid in training and in competition when it is used as a reminder or as an indicator to the wheelers, but it is a handicap when it gets caught in bushes and trees and I dare say that referees who have had whips thrust into their faces have their own views on the subject.

In training, a working whip capable of reaching the leaders and also strong enough to strike the wheelers firmly but not viciously is essential. The trouble with the traditional holly stick is that it is inclined to be brittle and is easily broken. A modern glass reinforced plastic stick with a nylon plaited thong or a lungeing whip, provided it has a thin handle, is perfectly adequate for training purposes. It is probably just as well to carry a full-length four-in-hand whip on the marathon carriage in case of need, but a light pairs whip is more practical, particularly in the hazards.

There are several reasons for using a whip in training. In the first place, a young horse meeting an unfamiliar situation is inclined to get anxious and may possibly shy, so that a touch with the whip before it feels like shying has the effect of distracting its attention and breaking the moment of tension. Secondly, it is necessary to remind an idle leader or wheeler to keep up with its neighbour. Some leaders will compete with the other to get ahead so that something has to be done to bring the more active horse back and to encourage the less active horse to keep up. Thirdly, one of the commonest problems is the wheeler that habitually drops back or pulls away as the pole comes towards it in a corner. This really aggravating and, on the marathon, dangerous habit can only be cured by a regular reminder of the need to keep up to the collar when on the inside of any turn. More points are lost in dressage and more disasters

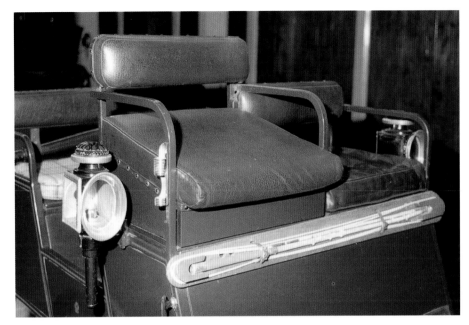

Spare whip in place on the best pony carriage. The whip holder can also be seen, convenient to the driver's right hand. (Alf. Baker)

are caused on the marathon by the inside wheeler dropping back in corners than for any other reason.

Professionals and purists will probably go pale with horror at the suggestion that during the competition the best thing to do with the thong of a whip is to tape it to the stick at the butt end and two-thirds of the way up, leaving the usual loop hanging from the far end. The point is that it would be much easier to drive without having to hold a whip in one hand at all, but it happens to be obligatory, therefore the best thing to do is to make sure that it gets in the way as little as possible. If you don't tape the end of the thong at the butt end, sooner or later it will get tangled up in the reins and that will be just enough to break your concentration or to delay your reaction by vital seconds.

The whip, taped to itself as described, is out of the way of the reins in a difficult manoeuvre. World Championships, Apeldoorn, 1982. (*Author's Collection*)

When they are giving marks for turnout during the dressage test, the judges are more likely to be impressed by a good old-fashioned knobbly holly stick whip with the thong coming off the top in a graceful curve. The only way to keep that curve is always to hang it on a proper whip roller when not in use and to treat it with great care, as the stick is connected with the thong by a goose quill which is easily broken. The leather thong should be kept supple with dubbin or some other leather dressing. Don't let anyone try to crack your best holly whip as they will surely break it.

There is a bit of an art in laying up a four-in-hand whip properly so that a loop hangs down from the outer end and the rest is wound round the stick with the lash end under the hand. The obvious way is to hold the lash end in the hand at the butt end with the whip vertically downwards and then twirl it round so that the thong winds its way up the stick for about two-thirds of its length. However, if you do it this way it puts a twist in the thong and when you hold it up you will find that the loop, instead of hanging tidily, will have twisted around itself.

It is almost impossible to describe the accepted way of laying up the turns on a whip, but the principle is to hold the lash under the right hand at the butt end with the whip horizontal, allowing the whole thong to hang in one loop. Then, by throwing the loop out sideways and catching it against the middle of the whip, the loop will wind itself on to the stick, half the turns going one way and half the other. The next thing is to hold the whip in the left hand at

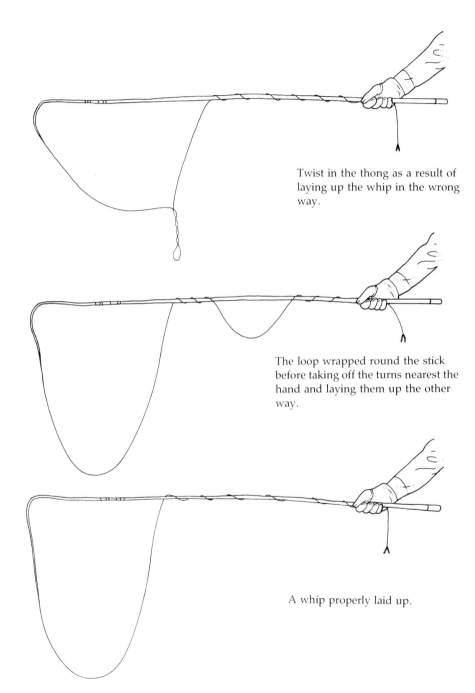

Twist in the thong as a result of laying up the whip in the wrong way.

The loop wrapped round the stick before taking off the turns nearest the hand and laying them up the other way.

A whip properly laid up.

the point where the turns reverse and with the right hand unlay the turns up to the middle and lay them up the other way, so that the thong forms a continuous spiral from the butt to two-thirds of the way up the stick. If you wondered why it was that a holly whip has those knobs on it, the answer now becomes apparent because they help to prevent the turns of the thong from sliding down the stick. To use the whip all you have to do is to hold it downwards or outwards and unwind the thong.

Finally the voice. Horses are great creatures of habit and it is therefore most important always to use the same words for the same purpose. It doesn't really matter what you say as long as the horses know exactly what you want them to do when you use a particular command and pre-ferably always in the same tone of voice. A flow of fruity language either before or after a com-mand may relieve your own tensions, but it will only confuse the horses and transfer the tensions to them.

Apart from giving commands to the team as a whole, there is a very great advantage in being able to talk to each horse individually. Therefore it is a good idea to use the horse's name when-ever you go up to it in the stable or give it a lump of sugar and to use soothing words so that it comes to associate them with calm and con-tentment. This can pay off handsomely in moments of stress later on. I once heard a lady say to her pony, as they approached an obstacle: 'Come on, Willie, you can read, first through A and then through B....'

Anyone who has listened to or experienced words of command on a parade ground will have noticed that there is always a slow warning word before the sharp word of command. It is just as well to use the same system with horses. If you want to move off or change pace, first get their attention by saying something like 'right, now', 'pay attention' or 'come along' before giving the order 'walk on' or 'trot'. Equally, before coming back from a trot to a walk or from a walk to a stop, some such introductory words as 'easy now' before the command to walk or halt gives the horses due warning. The same applies when you want the horses to back. The important thing is not to use the same warning as for forward movements. In other words, don't say 'pay attention – come back' because they will associate 'pay attention' with an order to move forward. Either use the word 'back' alone as you pull back on the reins or give a warning by saying 'come' slowly before 'back', provided, of course, you don't normally use the expression 'come along' to get them to go forward.

Some drivers can train their horses to respond correctly to 'come right' or 'come left' and this is obviously a great advantage, but in any case it is always worth saying 'come right' or 'come left' whenever you turn the horses as this will confirm to them the message they are getting from the reins.

In order to negotiate some of the more fiend-ishly complicated hazards dreamed up by sadistic course designers, it is very important to be able to get the leaders and/or the wheelers to move sideways or to come right round, one way or the other, without moving forwards. Wheelers should be trained to move sideways by a touch of the whip, a twitch of the rein and the order 'come over'. The leaders should be trained to 'fold' back by twitching the appropriate rein — as opposed to a steady pull — together with the words 'come round'.

While any movement or command is being properly executed it is a good idea to let the horses know that you are satisfied so that if anything goes wrong there is no doubt in their minds that you want them to stop by saying something like 'no' or 'stand still'.

As I have already said, it doesn't matter at all what words or sounds you use provided that you are scrupulously consistent and loud enough for the horses to hear you clearly. As a matter of fact there is a lot to be said for using unconventional words of command if only to prevent your horses responding to the words of another driver to his team standing nearby.

CHAPTER 7

GROOMS

At one time there was a separate competition for 'Presentation' in the International Rules. This was judged at the halt by special judges who inspected every bit of the carriage, harness and horses and gave marks accordingly. It was eventually done away with as the British always won this competition at international events. However, I believe it served its purpose in that it made competitors, and judges, go back to the authoritative books to discover exactly what was considered to be appropriate dress for the driver and grooms, and the correct combination of harness and carriage.

Under the current rules, ten marks are allowed for turnout in the dressage marking. It is not at all easy for the dressage judges to give much attention to turnout while they concentrate on accuracy, paces and all the other things they are supposed to judge. However, there is no point in giving away marks unnecessarily and a really good turnout does catch the judges' eyes. There are plenty of books on the subjects of stable management, grooming and turnout and anyone with experience of coaching classes or *concours d'élégance* will know exactly what to do to get good marks.

Feeding horses is a great art, particularly as no two horses need the same diet for the same amount of work. Furthermore the wrong diet can often be responsible for problems which do not appear to be related to diet. For instance, respiratory problems may be due to an allergy to hay or straw. Too much protein may give rise to foot problems. Not enough fibre may cause intestinal difficulties and so on.

Riding horses have certain problems due to the fact that they are carrying a body on their backs. Carriage horses are liable to other things. For instance, trotting fast, particularly over rough ground, almost invariably results in horses knocking their hooves together and this can often result in cuts on the coronet. Keep a careful watch for signs of this and fit coronet or fetlock protectors before any damage gets done. Then again, a carriage horse carries a lot of harness so keep a careful watch for any signs of rubbing.

Foam rubber taped to the harness or felt pads at the appropriate places can save a lot of trouble.

A navigator is needed on the marathon to keep track of the time, to help the driver keep to the right course and to remind him where to go in the hazards. Drivers remember these things in the normal course of events but if there is any problem with a horse the driver can easily get disorientated and lose track of the course or the next part of a hazard. A specialist navigator is a great help but in the long run it is probably better for these duties to be performed by someone who knows about horses because when things go wrong two people who can cope with horses and lift and push carriages are better than one.

At least one groom should know the dressage test as well as the driver. Again, under normal conditions, this may not be vital but the slightest drama with a horse can completely break the driver's concentration and by the time he has settled the problem with the horse he may well have lost the sequence of the test. It is, of course, strictly against the rules, but a ventriloquial hint from behind about the next movement is not easily detected by the judges and it will probably save the test from disaster.

Much the same applies during the obstacle driving and one of the grooms at least should walk the course with the driver and again a muttered 'left' or 'right' at the crucial moment or even the number of the next pair of cones can be a great help. However, on no account should a groom make any move to help the driver even so much as by getting up or moving his hands

as this will almost certainly be penalised by elimination.

For the marathon it is most important to have a standard plan of action for emergencies as well as a special plan for each particular section and hazard. The important point is that each groom must know what he is expected to do in various situations: where each groom will go when going down steep hills in order to make the brakes more effective; which position to take up to help to keep the carriage on four wheels when turning on a slope; which one will replace a broken trace, and so on. The most difficult decision is when to put the grooms down if things go wrong in a hazard, bearing in

The grooms should know where to be in case of emergencies. Ascot, 1986. (*Author's Collection*)

Grooms in their usual positions in an obstacle. (*Author's Collection*)

mind that while it costs twenty penalties to put both grooms down inside the hazard, every extra five seconds in it costs one penalty, therefore those twenty penalties are equivalent to one minute forty seconds and in terms of being stuck that is not a very long time. Getting the grooms down may be expensive, but it is less expensive than struggling for two minutes and of course it becomes even more expensive if you end up by having to put the grooms down anyway. The difficulty is to assess how seriously the carriage is stuck.

If the horses have got in a tangle, then one groom must go straight to the leaders' heads while the other sorts out the problem. If the carriage gets stuck it is almost invariably due to an obstruction getting between one of the wheelers and the splinter bar, or between the splinter bar and a front wheel. If the wheelers cannot move the carriage back and then move the pole across to get the obstruction clear of the wheel, they will have to be helped by one or both grooms. If the problem occurs on the flat, the wheelers can usually sort it out, but if the carriage is across a slope with the obstruction on the down side, things get a good deal more difficult.

In order to agree the special plan, one − the navigator − or preferably both grooms should accompany the driver on the reconnaissance of the marathon course and everyone must be agreed about the way in which each hazard is to be driven and what to do if things go wrong; always taking into consideration the particular problems of the hazard and the individual characteristics of each horse and the capacity of the team as a whole. There is nothing more frustrating, having got the grooms down in a hazard, to find that a groom is leading the horses the wrong way.

CHAPTER 8

BASIC TRAINING

This is not a book about 'ab-initio' breaking and training horses so I am going to take it that the horses you have chosen are rideable and broken to harness but otherwise rather green. The first thing to say is that the ridden instruction given to the horses is a vital preliminary to the instruction they will receive in harness. It is much easier to teach a horse to walk properly, to walk backwards and sideways and the difference between a collected, a working and an extended trot while mounted on its back than from a carriage, although a lot can be achieved with a horse in single harness. It is also, on the whole, less of a drama to ride a horse through water and to introduce it to such frightening monsters as tractors, diggers, bulldozers, traffic, cattle, dogs and lawn-mowers and more specifically the boards of a dressage ring, the obstacle cones and typical cross-country obstacles for the first time, while it is being ridden. Getting horses to go through water can be a problem in some cases. One way of getting over their reluctance is to wait for a

warm day and then to give the horse some strenuous exercise so that it gets good and hot and then take it to the water. A couple of lessons along these lines and most horses will come to associate water with a pleasant sensation. However, horses, being what they are, will happily go through a bit of water they know time and again, but choose to jib at a bit of water they have not seen before.

It is worth making a habit of rewarding the horses with sugar or carrots after each successful new accomplishment and particularly after practising dressage, obstacles and cones.

Even after this initiation process a regular carefree ride out is both good exercise and a welcome relief from the necessarily stricter discipline of pulling a carriage. Furthermore an occasional ride in pairs or in fours through dressage movements and between cones gives them a better idea of what you are asking them to do virtually on their own.

Having got the horses used to the sights and sounds they are likely to encounter while being

driven, and to the voice commands, the next step is to drive them out in pairs and to repeat all the lessons and to give them all the rewards they were given while being ridden.

If you look at any book about training horses – or any animals for that matter – they all agree that the art is to take only small steps at a time so that the next lesson never requires the horses to do anything radically different to its previous

experience, and always to repeat the last lesson before going on to the next. Some horses may appear to learn more quickly than others but the worst mistake is to take advantage of this and to try to advance more quickly than originally planned. Experience is vital and it needs to be built up bit by bit. It is easy enough to swallow a bit of food but that doesn't mean to say that it has been digested. If you go too fast the

To go well through water during a competition requires patient training at home. *(Alf. Baker)*

inevitable moment of indigestion will arrive and it will take much longer to get over such a set-back.

Before putting together as a team, the pairs of horses must have done virtually everything they will be required to do as a team. That means repeating everything they have done while being ridden. They must know the different paces and the basic movements of the dressage test. They must be able to back the carriage and hold it back while going down hills. They must have gone through water, sand and soft going without hesitation. They must have gone up and down hills, and twisted between trees and posts and rails. They must also have become used to passing between the cones and through the various types of multiple obstacles.

When it comes to training the horses to push the carriage backwards, always start on hard ground, facing slightly uphill, and have a groom by their heads. As they improve, get them to do it on the flat and only get them to back the carriage on grass or soft going when they are confident they can do it on a hard surface. When they are fully confident it is worth stopping and backing while practising in a hazard. This is something that is more than likely to be necessary during some event.

The only problem about driving horses in pairs is that some of the horses will not much like the pole. Most of them will probably learn to tolerate it with time and practice but some are never happy with it. With luck these will make better leaders, but not necessarily.

One very important point in the whole train-ing process is to establish a strict routine for setting off from the stables, whether the horses are being ridden or driven. In the first place they must learn to stand unattended for a few moments before being asked to walk on and then they should be patiently encouraged to walk quietly for the first ten or fifteen minutes. It may seem a hopeless task to begin with but slowly and by degrees they will get the message and this habit will pay handsome dividends in the future and the walk will also ensure that they are warmed up before beginning any harder work.

Having repeated all the basic lessons in pairs and having learnt something about the charac-ters of the horses, they can be put-to as a team. This will be rather a novel experience for the leaders and it is worth having several people on the ground walking beside them for the first few minutes. Once again the team should be put through all the basic lessons on the same principle of a little bit at a time. It is far better that they should feel faintly bored with the process than that they should lose confidence by being asked to do too much, too quickly. In any case the leaders have got to learn a whole new way of doing things. They must learn to come out of draft in corners, when going down-hill and in hazards. There is nothing more dangerous and hopeless than trying to drive a dressage test, or through hazards, or cones, with the leaders doing all the work. They must learn to judge by the tension on their traces where they are in relation to the wheelers, the swingle-trees and the pole. This is made more difficult for them as their blinkers prevent them seeing what is going on behind.

Equally the wheelers have to learn not to turn as soon as they see the leaders turning and only to come round in response to the rein. They have got to learn that they must cope with the whole weight of the carriage during most of the dressage test, in all the cross country hazards, through most of the cones, and to hold it back going down hills.

In theory every horse should be capable of going as a leader or a wheeler, and on either side, under all circumstances, but this is unlikely to be the case in practice. Some horses will go in the wheel if required but it may be that they go much better in the lead. Others may not

Leaders and wheelers must be trained to turn independently. *(Alf. Baker)*

have that slightly more adventurous and bolder nature to go in the lead and will be happier and more relaxed in the wheel. In any event it is always a good idea to move them around as much as possible, and to use the spare horse even though you have discovered what you think is the best way of putting them together. It prevents them getting 'one-sided' or into other habits that can come from always going with the same partner.

There are really two sides to the preparation of horses for competition. There is the training in speed and fitness and in ordinary carriage work, and there is the practice in the various elements of the competition. This practice is as important for the driver as it is for the horses and it is during these practice sessions that driver and horses begin to build up that absolutely essential mutual trust and confidence.

Every driver will have his own plan for training and practice depending on his circumstances: whether he has a special cross-country carriage as well as the 'best' carriage, and whether he is going to use the same arrangement of horses for each of the three parts of the competition or change them about.

In the event it will probably work out that, beginning with an initial period of exercise, practice for dressage and the cones will take place on one day and practice for the cross-country will be done on another, although it is perhaps best not to stick to such a routine too strictly, particularly if one or the other is presenting more problems. Furthermore, I have never come across any horse that appears to enjoy dressage practice, or driver, for that matter, and just a little too much of it will almost certainly take all the sparkle and impulsion out of the test itself. Ten minutes is quite long enough for a practice session. On the other hand, horses rather enjoy going through the cones and a bit too much practice can well lead to them becoming rather too enthusiastic. The equivalent of two rounds of an average course in any one session is probably about right.

While the individual parts of each outing should follow a strict routine, the outings themselves should be as varied as possible so as to keep the interest of the horses and prevent them going stale, but also bearing in mind that as the training proceeds the horses will be getting stronger and fitter and this must be matched by increasing their exercise in proportion.

It is quite a good idea to vary the length of the sessions depending on the amount of work done, but in principle it is probably enough to do not more than an hour a day for the first ten days to two weeks and then gradually to increase the sessions to between two and three hours, or two one and a half hour sessions, a day. It is a good idea to ride the horses out at least once a week and to give them a day off once a week.

CHAPTER 9

THE COMPETITION

Having acquired horses, harness and carriages, and trained the horses and yourself with the assistance of long-suffering grooms, the next step seems obvious enough – enter for a competition. Nothing, however, is more apt to driving than the saying 'There is many a slip 'twixt the cup and the lip'. Anyone with experience of horses knows that they are prone to an almost unlimited number of diseases and injuries which are liable to make them unusable when you most need them. If something or other has not happened to your horses to make you wish that you had never started on the whole thing, you would be the one great exception.

However, assuming that you have come through breakdown, accident, sickness, injury, temperament and act of God, and it really looks as if you might get to a competition, a whole new set of problems looms up on the horizon.

The first thing to remember is that organising committees don't just accept anyone who turns up. There have been cases of competitors who have turned up without having entered and

pleading with the judges to be allowed to go *hors concours*, though why we use a French expression for 'outside the competition' I'm not quite sure. Committees expect formal entries to be made and, if it is an international event, the entry must be made through your National Equestrian Federation. They will demand FEI horse passports properly filled in, together with valid certificates for any obligatory vaccinations or inoculations that may be in force at the time. So it is worth reading the entry forms carefully and filling them in accurately. Committees are fairly tolerant, but it is very easy to get a bad reputation and it is very irritating to have to pay a fine.

The next problem is to get the whole circus of five horses, three grooms, yourself, plus two or three extra helpers, two carriages, two sets of harness, rugs, feed, grooming and medical equipment, whips and the thousand and one other items, from home to the place of the event. For transport there are a number of permutations: a five-horse box plus a vehicle with a loading

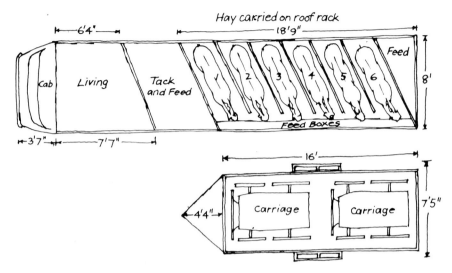

George Bowman's horsebox and carriage trailer, 1981 season. (*Ray Manning*)

ramp capable of taking two carriages plus harness boxes and hampers with all the other kit. Then you and your grooms will need accommodation, preferably not too far from the horses. This can be provided by a caravan or accommodation can be fitted into the front end of the horse box. An articulated tug and trailer can provide reasonable accommodation plus room for the horses and all their kit. This leaves the carriages to be transported on their own trailer behind another vehicle. It is equally possible to fit accommodation and horses into a big horse box and then tow a trailer with the carriages and kit behind it. Even with this arrangement you will still need some sort of car – preferably four-wheel-drive – for general use and particularly for driving round the course.

The main danger on arrival is the parking area. British weather being what it is, the chances are that you will arrive in blazing sunshine and park on lovely hard turf. However, it is more than likely that before the weekend is out there will have been a cloudburst and moving horse boxes and other heavy vehicles will become virtually impossible without the help of tractors. Reconnaissance and forethought are seldom wasted before settling on a place to park. This is particularly important if you make use of a tent fitted to the side of the box as temporary stabling.

TURNOUT

Turnout is judged as part of the dressage test, but the requirements are quite different to the rest of the test. Judges, of course, vary in their views but generally speaking marks go for cleanliness and correctness. Needless to say, what the judges believe to be correct, or the importance they attach to any particular item, may not have quite the same significance in the driver's opinion or in that of his grooms.

The most difficult part in producing a good turnout is to find four matching horses, or even two matching leaders and two matching wheelers, that are also capable of doing a reasonable dressage test. It is one of those facts of fate that if you have two slightly larger and two slightly smaller horses, one of the larger will not go in the wheel and one of the smaller will not go in the lead. Furthermore, if you can find a horse without any blemish or scar or allergy or some other maddening idiosyncrasy, like not standing still at the halt in the dressage test or persistently nagging its neighbour, you will be very lucky indeed.

The points that count are the matching and cleanliness of the horses, and this includes the condition of their hooves and shoes; properly pulled tails; correctly plaited manes; and clean ears, eyes and nose, and the other orifices.

Next in importance is the condition and fit of the harness. It is easy enough, although expensive, to get a set of beautiful harness but it won't score any points if it isn't properly fitted. Particular attention needs to be paid to the fit of the collars and the hames of the collars; the fit of the bridles and bits; the fit of the back pad so

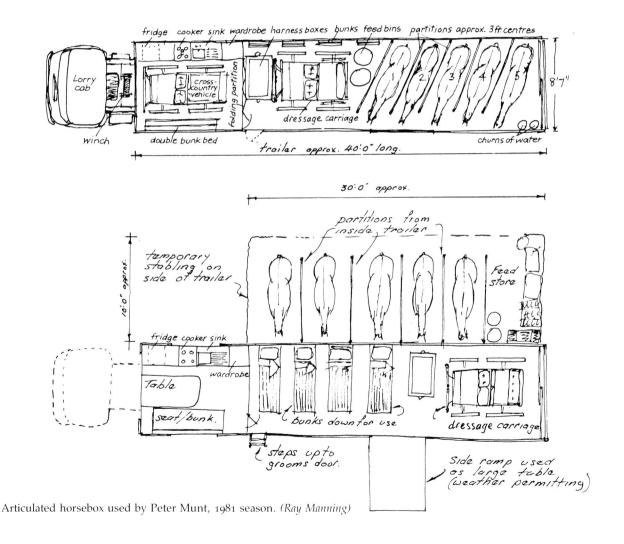

Articulated horsebox used by Peter Munt, 1981 season. *(Ray Manning)*

that there is a space over the spine; the length of the traces and the pole-chains; the height of the pole and the attachment of the swingle-trees and leaders' traces.

The cleanliness of the carriage is obviously important, and really shiny brightwork always stands out. The carriage also needs to be appropriate to the size of the horses and to the style of the harness. Points to remember are the lamps and rear lamps and the clothing and turnout of the grooms.

The aim of the driver should be to choose an appropriate outfit, including shoes, that matches, blends or contrasts with his horses, carriage and grooms so that the whole turnout makes a pleasing and harmonious impression.

CHAPTER 10

DRESSAGE

There are really two parts to this competition. There is the test of driving skill and accuracy and there is the performance of the horses — the way they hold themselves, their paces, impulsion, regularity and suppleness. A driver can do a certain amount about the latter, by training and particularly by riding the horses, but he has to do everything about the former.

Accuracy in the figures depends absolutely on the driver's control of the wheelers and all the time and patience spent on getting the inside wheeler to go into its collar in the corners is never wasted. The leaders obviously have their part to play in stopping, starting and transitions from one movement to the next; however, the wheelers provide the controlling power. In fact it is not at all a bad idea to practise dressage movements just with the pair of wheelers. I suggest only the movements and not the test as a whole because horses learn a routine very quickly and they have a nasty habit of anticipating the next move. The worst of all

is to practise so much that the horses get bored with the whole thing. There is nothing more frustrating than to go into the arena all keyed up and ambitious only to find that the horses have lost interest and gone to sleep. On the other hand, it requires a fine judgement to get horses that are fit and strong enough for the marathon to be sufficiently calm and manageable for the dressage. A warm up before the dressage is essential but too much can be just as unsatisfactory as too little.

The clue to dressage is total concentration on the test but this means that if anything unexpected happens to break that concentration, such as a horse shying or behaving stupidly, or you start thinking about something else, like how well you are doing, it is very easy to lose track of the test and for your mind to go blank. This is where the ventriloquial groom can save you from disaster.

I have already described the method of buckling the reins together. The period of the warm up should be used to make certain that the reins

are in the right holes for the particular horses being used and for the mood they happen to be in on the day.

The problem with most teams is holding off the wheelers in the corners rather than turning the leaders. One way of holding off the wheelers in a right-handed circle or corner is to slip the near wheeler rein over your left thumb. Unfortunately it is not quite so easy to do the same with the off wheeler rein, but it can be achieved with practice, if necesssary. A touch of the whip on the inside wheeler helps but it is very difficult to do this without momentarily releasing the pressure on the reins unless the opposition rein is over the thumb.

An important factor in driving accurate figures is to know where you are in the arena and where you ought to be. Although the arena has right angle corners, it is obviously impossible to drive a right angle. However, you will notice that the arena is 40 m wide, consequently in order to drive down one side and then turn up the middle you have, in effect, to make a turn on a half circle with a radius of approximately 10 m (approximately because while the centre of the carriage travels about 1.5 m inside the boards it runs over the centre line of the arena).

The rules state that the change of movement should take place 'at the time the leaders reach the point indicated on the test' (1980) and this applies to all halts and transitions, but it cannot apply to turns. For example, if you are required to describe a half-circle beginning at B and ending at X and you start to turn your leaders as they reach B the carriage will have started the

turn before it reaches B, consequently you will not be able to describe an accurate half-circle and get the centre of the carriage to pass over X. You would have an even more difficult job to get the carriage to pass over D if you started to turn the leaders at K.

It so happens that all the turns and circles (except for the 30 m diameter circles) have to be driven as if on a circle of 10 m radius. Therefore, when going into a corner the leaders have to be turned at a point which will allow the front wheels of the carriage to start to turn as they reach the marker 10 m from the corner.

This means that the leaders and then the wheelers should only start to be turned, not as they reach the marker, but as they pass it. This should ensure that the carriage wheels describe a smooth arc along the circumference of a circle with a radius of 10 m that touches both the side and the end boards. One way of practising turns and circles is to put a plastic cone about 2.5 m in from the boards opposite the turning point marker and two cones about 1.5 m either side of point D. Alternatively you can mark the track to be followed by the centre of the carriage with a trail of sawdust.

In order to get the movements right in the test itself it is just as well to make a reconnaissance of the arena before the competition so as to get an idea of the relationship of the arena boards and markers to the surrounding landscape. This is particularly important when it comes to executing loops and circles accurately. Most tests include a series of loops to and fro across the arena, and if you look at the marking of the

(opposite page) HRH The Duke of Edinburgh driving the dressage test with the team of Fells, Royal Windsor Horse Show. *(Alf. Baker)*

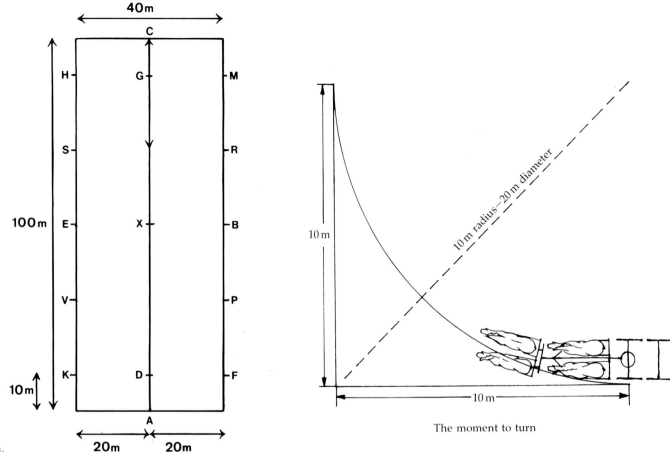

40m

C

H   G   M

S   R

100m   E   X   B

V   P

K   D   F

A

10m

10m

20m   20m

Dressage arena.

10 m

10 m radius—20 m diameter

10 m

The moment to turn

(opposite page) The team of bays competing in the dressage at Brighton.

arena you will notice that each loop consists of a semi-circle of 20 m diameter, with the boards forming a tangent to the middle of each loop. This means that the 'straights' across the arena between the loops should be half way between the turning points.

Judicious use of the footbrake can also help. Horses go more evenly if the load on the traces remains fairly constant, therefore, a touch on the brakes when slowing down or going into corners or stopping makes things easier for the wheelers. However, the brake should be used with care; it does not make a good impression if most of the test is done with the back wheels locked and, in many cases, the use of the brake only makes some horses pull even harder.

Apart from getting the figures as accurate as possible, it is very important to get the horses to do the paces required. Whatever the purists may say, the extended trot has the effect of making the carriage go faster so that acceleration to the extension is important. There is very little

time, even on a diagonal, to work up to an extension. The working trot has to be active but it also needs to be seen to be slower than the extended trot. As a matter of fact, a working trot is about as fast as most horses can get round the corners in a dignified manner. This leaves the collected trot which must be seen to be slower and more deliberate than the working trot. The trouble, of course, is that a slow and measured collected trot is about the most soporific activity you can invite a horse to do. On the other hand it is virtually impossible to get pulling horses to do a circle at the collected trot with the reins in one hand. I don't think there is a best way to drive a circle, but in principle it is necessary to take a loop of exactly the right size and then to increase or decrease the pull by moving your whole arm to the left or to the right. If the loop slips or if a leader takes it into its head to make for the boards in the second half you are in trouble.

It is worth remembering that the style of the driver is also being judged, therefore it is important to try to sit up straight and to look calm and relaxed whatever may be happening inside. In fact, you have to behave rather like a swan moving away from danger – all calm and serene on the surface but paddling like hell underneath.

CHAPTER 11

THE MARATHON

This quite inappropriately named competition (after all, Pheidippides ran from Marathon to Athens on his feet) is the most important in a combined driving event. Roughly speaking the relative value of each competition works out at about 3 for the dressage, 10 for the marathon and 1 for the cones. Therefore the time spent on practising for the hazards and for the speeds required is never wasted.

The marathon consists of five sections. Section A is supposed to be over roads and tracks, but it can include water crossings, hills and tight turns. Section B is the first walk of about 1 km and is supposed to be along a flat and hard surface. Then there is a ten-minute halt, when the horses may be inspected by a vet. Section C is fairly short, but at a fast trot, and Section D is the second walk, which is again followed by a ten-minute halt and an inspection. Section E is supposed to be at an ordinary trot, but as it includes up to eight hazards, the tendency is to go rather faster than necessary in case of a hold-up in the hazards.

Speed is important for two reasons. Section C demands a fairly high average speed and to achieve an average means being able to reach a top speed at least 10 per cent faster than the average demanded, in order to compensate for corners, hills, rough going and so on. To achieve an average of 18 kph your team needs to be able to do at least 20 kph. In any event it is virtually impossible to keep to a steady speed on all sections of the course.

Secondly, although the average speed in Section E may not be particularly fast, there is always the chance of getting stuck in a hazard or of some other misfortune so that time in hand can sometimes come in very useful.

There may be some infallible way of getting horses to trot faster without breaking into a canter, but if there is I haven't found it. It is sometimes possible to get them to realise that they are able to go a lot faster than they think they can by getting them to trot towards home as quickly as possible, but this method depends on the temperament of the horses.

It is no good trying this method if it only makes them pull, and in any case they may not have discovered where home is at a competition. If the competition happens to be at their home ground, the problem is more likely to be how to get them to go away from their stables.

The walk sections sound fairly straightforward but 7 kph (6 kph for ponies) is quite a fast walk and few horses achieve it without a great deal of patient practice and considerable urging.

The secret about driving the hazards is study. Some hazards may offer no options, in which case it is very important to decide exactly what you are going to do with the reins and the horses and at which precise moment; always bearing in mind the individual characteristics of the horses — particularly of the wheelers.

Be very careful about judging a hazard entirely by eye. Optical illusions can make certain hazards look much easier or more difficult than

The pony team in the water obstacle at the International Driving Event, Royal Windsor Horse Show. (*Alf. Baker*)

they are in practice. For instance, at a distance gaps look much narrower than they really are. It is therefore very important to get the line of approach exactly right even if it looks impossible from a distance.

In judging any hazard it is worth bearing in mind that only the most brilliant, or perhaps the luckiest, drivers can get through a zig-zag route that requires the leaders to be going one way, the wheelers to be going another and the carriage yet another all at the same time. Therefore when in doubt look for somewhere to loop.

Whereas it may be necessary in some cases to stop the horses in a hazard so as to position them for the next gate, there are other occasions when to stop is to court disaster. In other words, there are some situations in which it is essential to keep the horses moving — particularly the wheelers in order to get past critical turning points.

Hazards that offer a number of options need a great deal of study so as to arrive at the fastest driveable route. Naturally it depends a lot on the size of the horses, but a good general rule is that it is quicker to choose a route that keeps the whole team moving rather than a shorter route that demands stopping and side-stepping and the risk of getting stuck on a corner. It is very important to know the number of paces between the box seat and the leaders' heads and also the length of the pole so that during the study of a hazard you can pace out the distances to get an idea where the pole end and the leaders will be when you need to turn the wheelers. It is always a good idea to take as much room as possible by keeping as far out in a turn as you can and to try to get the front wheel past the critical corner before allowing the wheelers to come round. It is safer to aim for a sharper turn than to turn too soon and get a front wheel caught on a post or a tree.

Always bear in mind that while there appears to be plenty of room when you are looking at a hazard on your feet, the place becomes very crowded as soon as four horses and a carriage get into it. One factor easily overlooked is that while even the wheelers can bend and move about relative to the pole, the pole itself is rigidly attached to the carriage and sticks out in front by some ten feet. This means that in certain circumstances it is physically impossible to take a carriage through a particular gap simply because there is no room for the pole to swing round. For example, if there is limited room to pull out in order to turn at right angles through a gate off a lane, the pole will either strike the far gate post or the inside front wheel will come up against the near gate post. In such a case the best thing to do is to get the carriage as far out from the gap as possible and to drive the leaders well past the gap and then stop so that the wheelers can get through the gap. The idea is to get the leaders to come back a step or two and then to put them through the gap and hopefully to get the whole outfit through diagonally. Quite a good method of judging the minimum diagonal angle is to have a stick equal in length to the track width of your carriage. By laying the stick on the ground with one end against the critical obstruction you can get an idea of the angle of

A variety of early solutions to the marathon vehicle problem. *(Jack Watmough)*

approach necessary to get through the gap. Even so it is always safer to aim to hit the outside obstruction rather than the one on the inside of the turn.

There will be many hazards where it is impossible to go direct from one pair of flags to the next. In these cases it is necessary to go through the first pair and to go out and circle round for the next pair. The choice of which way to turn depends on a number of factors, but the most important one is the angle at which you want to arrive at the next pair of flags. In principle it is easier to keep turning the horses on the same rein whenever possible. It is also worth bearing in mind that it is usually easier to steer the wheelers accurately when going uphill rather than downhill when their traces will be slack, so that if there is a choice it is better to loop in such a way that you approach the gates of a hazard going uphill, provided, of course, that it is possible to go straight through the gate without having to turn the leaders before the carriage is at least half way through the gate.

Remember that in turning on the side of a slope the wheelers are more inclined to drop down the hill into the corner than they would on the flat, therefore it is necessary to go further than usual before turning. Remember also that the leaders can usually be expected to go into their collars going uphill so that when turned they are likely to pull the end of the pole around. This can be quite embarrassing if you have to turn sharply uphill in a hazard. Bear in mind that while you have seen the hazards and decided on a route, the whole thing will be new to the horses and, if an obvious gap presents itself to the leaders, they will naturally tend to make for it. Some intelligent horses seem to be able to recognise red and white markers but I would not rely on it.

Going down a steep slope it is very difficult to prevent the wheelers from accelerating, even though the brakes are full on, so that it is wise to start the descent slowly, and straight in order to prevent jack-knifing. Make sure that you have shortened the wheelers' reins because when the

Holding off the wheelers with the right hand while turning the leaders with the loop in the left hand.
(Alf. Baker)

wheelers sit back in their breeching to hold the carriage back their heads can come something like two feet closer to your hand and you will find that even with your hands beside your ears you are still not making much impression.

Water crossings are more spectacular than they are hazardous, provided, of course, the horses have had plenty of practice and that none of them shows any persistent reluctance or hesitation about going into water. Even so it is as well not to surprise horses by rushing them round a corner or over a steep bank at a water crossing as the leaders usually need a moment or two to adjust to the situation. It is worth remembering that as the leaders go in, the water is inclined to slow them down, therefore if the carriage is going too fast the wheelers and the pole are liable to run up close behind the leaders, and then if one of the leaders tries to duck away from the water it is virtually impossible to do anything about it while it is off the bit. The other danger is that the swingle-trees will be hanging down and if a wheeler plunges forward as it goes into the water it may well get a leg over one of the bars. Therefore in general it is best to go into water relatively slowly so as to give the leaders a chance to get into the water and into draught before increasing the pace again.

Before starting on the marathon it is as well to check that you have all the necessary spares with you and stowed in the right places and

The Fell pony team coming out of the Tay at Scone Palace. *(Alf. Baker)*

that they are all compatible with the harness and carriage in use. It is no use taking spare clip-on traces if the swingle-trees are designed for running-loop traces. In addition there are several other items of equipment that are worth including: a sharp knife large enough to cut through the traces; plenty of harness tape; at least four halter ropes; some stout 'washing line' type of rope; and adjustable spanner, hammer, screwdriver and any other appropriate tools.

As for the horses, some people believe in tying up their tails as for polo ponies. It helps to prevent the leaders getting their tails over the reins. It is certainly a good idea to fit the horses with lightweight head collars under their bridles. None of these precautions may be needed but as with anything to do with horses, things do go wrong when they are least expected.

Contrary to first impressions, it is better to give the leaders longer than normal traces for the marathon. As I have already explained, the point is that it is quite often necessary to 'fold back' the leaders but if their traces are short this cannot be done without pulling the end of the pole round or bringing the leaders right back on the wheelers. There is a risk of getting a leg over a trace but with trace carriers and short-coupled swingle-trees it is not a serious one.

I have already described the method of two-handed driving. For all the sections other than E (with the hazards), the difference between the length of the leader and wheeler reins need be no more than sufficient to get the leaders just out of draught when the wheelers are feeling the reins. For the hazards it is just as well to shorten the wheelers by one hole and the leaders by two holes. The reason is that it is impossible to drive complicated obstacles with the leaders in draught and with sharp corners you need to pull in a lot of rein.

The shortened reins may mean that, on occasions such as during a walk, the driver has to lean further forward than strictly elegant but the practical advantage is far more important.

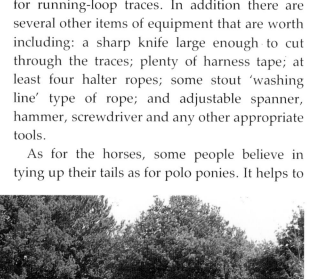

In one of the obstacles during the marathon at the World Championships, 1986, Ascot. (*Author's Collection*)

TIMEKEEPING AND NAVIGATION

As the whole marathon is a 'time trial' it is worth taking trouble to ensure that you arrive at the end of each section at the right time. Sections A, C and E are marked with kilometre markers, so that it is only necessary to work out at what time − or after what interval of time − each marker should be reached. If there is any doubt about the exact length of any section, it is much more important to get the last part of the section right than the first. It may not always be convenient, but where possible it is worth checking the positions of the last two kilometre markers of each section, particularly if the last bit is less than a full kilometre.

To avoid having to work out on each occasion the time for each kilometre at different speeds, it is quite a good idea to make out a conversion table for speeds from say 12 to 20 kph and for distances up to 15 km. It is then a simple matter to look up the times at the appropriate distances for the appropriate speeds.

It is probably best to put down the distances and times for each section on a separate piece of paper. Some people use the backs of envelopes, others use rather more elaborate forms clipped to a board, but as long as the navigator produces the right answer and can tell the driver how fast or slow the team is against the clock, the method employed is not important.

There are two basic methods of timing. You can use an ordinary stop watch, preferably with a 'split-timer', and start it at the beginning of each section. By using the 'split' button as you pass the markers you can read off the time and note it down and then by pressing it again the watch reverts to the elapsed time. The other system is to use a watch which shows the time of day, but which is also fitted with a 'split' time facility. This type of watch needs to be set correctly on either the radio or the 'talking clock' time signal before the competition. This type of watch is used by the timekeepers on the ground so that it is easier to check any errors or mis-understandings and it also makes it possible to relate progress to the overall time-table. The only snag is that your time-table is liable to be

Speed−time−distance tables

Speed kph

	14		15		16		17		18		19		
	Min	Sec	Min	Sec	Min	Sec	Min	Sec	Min	Sec	Min	Sec	
0.5	2	08	2		1	52	1	46	1	40	1	35	0.5
1	4	16	4		3	44	3	32	3	20	3	10	1
1.5	6	24	6		5	36	5	18	5		4	45	1.5
2	8	32	8		7	28	7	04	6	40	6	20	2
2.5	10	40	10		9	20	8	50	8	20	7	55	2.5
3	12	48	12		11	12	10	36	10		9	30	3
3.5	14	56	14		13	04	12	22	11	40	11	05	3.5
4	17	04	16		14	56	14	08	13	20	12	40	4
4.5	19	12	18		16	48	15	54	15		14	15	4.5
5	21	20	20		18	40	17	40	16	40	15	50	5
5.5	23	28	22		20	32	19	26	18	20	17	25	5.5
6	25	36	24		22	24	21	12	20		19	00	6
6.5	27	44	26		24	16	22	58	21	40	20	35	6.5
7	29	52	28		26	08	24	44	23	20	22	10	7
7.5	32	00	30		28	00	26	30	25		23	45	7.5
8	34	08	32		29	52	28	16	26	40	25	20	8
8.5	36	16	34		31	44	30	02	28	20	26	55	8.5
9	38	24	36		33	36	31	48	30		28	30	9
9.5	40	32	38		35	28	33	34	31	40	30	05	9.5
10	42	40	40		37	20	35	20	33	20	31	40	10
10.5	44	48	42		39	12	37	06	35		33	15	10.5
11	47	56	44		41	04	38	52	36	40	34	50	11
11.5	49	04	46		42	56	40	38	38	20	36	25	11.5
12	51	12	48		44	48	42	24	40		38	00	12
12.5	53	20	50		46	40	44	10	41	40	39	35	12.5
13	55	28	52		48	32	45	56	43	20	41	10	13
13.5	57	36	54		50	24	47	42	45		42	45	13.5
14	59	44	56		52	16	49	28	46	40	44	20	14

Distance km

kph	12		13		14		15		16		17		18		19	
Metres	Min	Sec	Min	Sec	Min	Sec	Min	Sec	Min	Sec	Min	Sec	Min	Sec	Min	Sec
500	2	30	2	15	2	05	2		1	50	1	46	1	40	1	35
400	2		1	48	1	40	1	36	1	28	1	25	1	20	1	16
300	1	30	1	21	1	15	1	12	1	06	1	03	1			57
200	1			54		50		48		44		42		40		38
100		30		27		25		24		22		21		20		19
50		15		13.5		12.5		12		11.0		10.6		10		9.5
10		3		2.7		2.5		2.4		2.2		2.1		2		1.9

kph	12	13	14	15	16	17	18	19
Metres/Minute	200	216.5	233.5	250	266.5	283.5	300	316.5
Metres/Second	3.33	3.61	3.88	4.16	4.44	4.72	5.0	5.27

Time difference per kilometre

	12		13		14		15		16		17		18		19
13		24													
14		42		18											
15	1			36		18									
16	1	15		51		33		15							
17	1	30	1	06		48		20		15					
18	1	42	1	18	1			42		27		12			
19	1	51	1	27	1	09		51		36		21		09	

10 kph − 166.6 mpm − 2.77 mps

Metres	10	20	30	40	50	100	200	300
Seconds	3.6	7.2	10.8	14.4	18	36	72	108

7 kph − 116.6 mpm − 1.94 mps

Metres	10	50	100	200	300	400	500	600	700	800	900	1000
Seconds	5.15	25.7	51.5	1 43	2 34	3 26	4 17	5 09	6	6 52	7 4	8 35

confused if, for some reason, one of your start times is changed at the last minute.

There is one danger in using 'split-timers' on watches with 'analogue' faces (i.e. conventional clock face) as opposed to watches with a 'digital' read out. While the 'split' second hand stops when you press the 'split' button, the minute hand goes on. Consequently if you stop the 'split' hand a few seconds before the full minute, by the time you have noted the seconds the other second hand and the minute hand will have passed the minute and it is very easy to add an extra minute in this way. This cannot happen with a digital watch.

One of the most vital functions of the navigator/timekeeper is to keep track of the compulsory red and white numbered turning flags and to remind the driver of any particularly tricky or difficult bits along the course. Drivers have quite enough to do merely concentrating on the horses and on the going immediately in front of them and they may therefore easily forget a sudden change of course. It is surprising how many experienced drivers have been eliminated for failing to notice a compulsory turning flag.

Needless to say no course is so laid out that it is possible to drive it all at the required average speed. There is therefore a need to plan where time can be made up and where time is likely to be lost. There is no point, however, in rushing the early part on principle, and then finding it necessary to dawdle at the end. Since there are two minutes between minimum and maximum times in Section A, the aim should be to arrive

more or less halfway between the two on the middle minute. In Section C the allowance is only 1 minute, so the aim should be to arrive 30 seconds after the minimum time. There is no minimum time in Section E, so it is only necessary to try to finish within the maximim time allowed for the section.

The most difficult section from the timekeeping point of view is the section (E) incorporating the hazards. The course designer measures each section and adjusts the overall distance so that a whole number of minutes is required at the chosen average speed, or he may simply 'round up' the time to the nearest minute. For example the actual time required to cover 8 500 m at an average speed of 16 kph is 31 minutes 52 seconds. Therefore the course designer can either allow 32 minutes or he can add 30 m to the course and make it 8 530 m to be done in 32 minutes.

The trouble arises in Section E because, even though the course designer includes the distances within the hazards in the overall measurement of the section, it is not possible to drive through the average hazard at the average speed allowed for the section as a whole. For example, if Section E is measured at 8 500 m and is to be driven at an average speed of 15 kph, the time allowed would be 34 minutes. However, the section includes up to eight hazards and the record suggests that, in major competitions, a rough average for the time spent in a hazard is about one minute, although actual times may vary widely depending on the distance between the entry and exit gates and the complication and number of gates within an individual hazard.

Since there is no minimum time for Section E, the only requirement is to get to the finish within the maximum time allowed. This would cause no more difficulty than Sections A and C, except for the eight hazards. Apart from the fact that you are unlikely to be able to drive through a hazard at the average speed required for the whole section, there is the added possibility that you may get temporarily stuck in one or more of the hazards. The Rules state that you are eliminated if you spend more than five minutes in a hazard, so almost the worst case would be if you took, say, four minutes in each hazard. That would add up to 32 minutes and however fast you drove you would be bound to be late at the finish. Therefore the art in timing Section E is to go fast enough to allow yourself some extra time in case you get stuck, but not so fast that you exhaust the horses.

The problem for the navigator is to be able to estimate how far ahead or behind schedule you are at each kilometre marker. It would be easy enough to add a time allowance for the hazards as a whole, but unfortunately the hazards do not come conveniently every 1 000 m. Consequently, it will obviously take longer to drive a kilometre with two hazards in it than one without any.

The essential calculation depends on the extra time you will need to get through a hazard. For example, if the distance through a hazard is 150 m, it would take 36 seconds at 15 kph. If you managed to drive it at 10 kph, it would take 54

seconds. The difference is 18 seconds. If there are eight hazards in the course, the total time difference − provided there were no hold-ups − would be a little under two and a half minutes. Therefore, if you drove the bits of the course between the hazards at 15 kph, and the hazards at 10 kph, you would be nearly two and a half minutes late. If you take the two and a half minutes off the 34 minutes allowed, it comes to 31 minutes 30 seconds, and that means that you would have to drive at just over 16 kph between the hazards. If you then want to get some time in hand in case of hold-ups, you will have to drive that much faster.

Assuming the section measures 8 500 m and the time allowed is 34 minutes (15 kph), you would have to allow four minutes per kilometre. However, in every kilometre with a hazard, you would have to go 18 seconds faster. If there were two hazards in a kilometre you would have to go 36 seconds faster to maintain your schedule. If you wanted to get some time in hand, you would have to go faster still. It takes four minutes to cover one kilometre at 15 kph and 3 minutes 20 seconds to cover it at 18 kph. If you aimed to drive at 18 kph between the hazards and added the two and a half minutes for the time spent in the hazards, and provided you were not held up, you ought to finish with over three minutes in hand.

Say the course measures 8 500 m and you decide to drive the bits between the eight hazards at 18 kph, and, say, the hazards are spaced as follows: no hazards in the first kilometre, numbers 1 and 2 in the second kilometre, number 3

Section . . . .   Page . . . .   Distance . . . .   Average   Speed . . . .

Start (Time of day) Hrs Min	Max time allowed Min	Time to finish (Time of day) Hrs Min	Minimum time for section A. 2 minutes less than time allowed
			Minimum time for section C: 1 minute less than time allowed

Position	Distance Km	Time allowed Min Sec	Time taken Min Sec	
Start To				

No	Time allowed	Time taken	Penalties	No	Time allowed	Time taken	Penalties	
1				5				
2				6				
3				7				
4				8				

in the third, numbers 4 and 5 in the fourth, none in the fifth, none in the sixth, numbers 6 and 7 in the seventh, and number 8 in the eighth kilometre. The time plan would then look something like this:

Km	Hazard	Accumulative time		
1	none	3 m 20 s		
2	1 & 2	+3 m 20 s = 6 m 40 s + 2 × 18 s	= 7 m 16 s	
3	3	+3 m 20 s = 10 m 36 s + 18 s	= 10 m 54 s	
4	4 & 5	+3 m 20 s = 14 m 14 s + 2 × 18 s	= 14 m 50 s	
5	none	+3 m 20 s	= 18 m 10 s	
6	none	+3 m 20 s	= 21 m 30 s	
7	6 & 7	+3 m 20 s = 24 m 50 s + 2 × 18 s	= 25 m 26 s	
8	8	+3 m 20 s = 28 m 46 s + 18 s	= 29 m 4 s	
+500 m	none	+1 m 40 s	= 30 m 44 s	

Whatever time you choose to arrive it is absolutely vital to agree with the navigator beforehand about which finishing time is going to be used. There is a considerable difference between being 30 seconds slow on maximum time, 30 seconds slow on the middle minute or 30 seconds slow on minimum time. Thirty seconds slow on maximum time means six penalty points and 30 seconds fast on minimum time means three penalty points. Therefore, working on the middle minute or half minute gives the greatest latitude for error either way.

Timekeeping does not help much in the walk section as it is always a matter of walking as fast as possible. Nothing is more dangerous than to assume that the horses can always make it. The going varies, the measurements may not be absolutely accurate and the horses may be feeling different on the day. A check point half-way along the section can give an idea of how they are going, but whatever the time at half-way it is never wise to relax the urging for an instant. Most walk sections take about 10 minutes and they are the longest 10 minutes of any marathon.

CHAPTER 13

OBSTACLES

The two most important factors in driving an obstacle course are practice and re-connaissance. If you can drive through about eighteen pairs of cones set at 30 cm wider than the track width of your carriage, without touching any of them while practising, you should be able to do the same in a competition. The only difference is that the competition course will not be the same as the practice course and that is why walking the course is so important. The problem is always to visualise what the various obstacles and turns will look like from the box seat and moving at about three times walking speed. In principle you should aim to turn the team in such a way that it is going in a straight line for at least one length before reaching the next pair of cones. In order to achieve this it is quite possible that you will have to turn slightly away from the next pair so as to give yourself room to straighten out before the leaders get to the next cones. This is all right in theory but if it means taking the horses close to the spectators it may not be as easy as it sounds particularly if

(opposite page) Straight through the cones. Team of Fells at Stanmer Park. *(Alf. Baker)*

someone opens a striped umbrella at that exact moment and when you know that one of the leaders has an aversion to striped umbrellas. It is quite possible to go through a pair of cones at an angle or while turning but it is obvious that you will always get the widest possible gap if you go through exactly at right angles to the two cones.

L and U shaped obstacles look more daunting than they are in practice, provided always that you take full advantage of all the space available by skirting the outside edge of the obstacle. That is to say, if the L or U shaped obstacle is to the right you should aim to enter the obstacle as far over to the left as possible, turning the leaders as late as you can and holding off the wheelers until you are certain that the carriage will clear the corner. It also helps to touch the brakes on the way in and then to release them as the wheelers get to the corner so that the sudden relaxation on their traces encourages them to go on just that vital pace before turning to follow the leaders. This may sound rather exaggerated,

but it only needs one of the wheelers to take a sudden step sideways or for the inside wheeler to drop back and without a bit of extra room you will hit the corner cone.

Having watched a good many people driving obstacle courses I have come to the conclusion that many drivers feel that they will do better if they go slowly and carefully. Carefully yes, but there is no point in going slowly when it is not necessary. Try walking the team through a series of obstacles and you will find that it is more difficult than trotting. Two hundred metres a minute, or 12 kph, may not sound very fast but it is surprising how you have to keep going to make the time, particularly if it is a tight course. There are some places in a course where it is obviously important to slow down but there are other parts where the team might just as well move on a bit more quickly. Needless to say it all depends on the handiness and responsiveness of the team. If the leaders are chronic pullers the chances of a clear round are remote, but if the wheelers are active and biddable and the leaders don't pull, the chances are much better.

Once the team is lined up and going straight for an obstacle it is less likely to make a sudden deviation if it is going on fairly smartly than if you are struggling to hold it back. It is rather like show-jumping where the rider slows and steadies his horse between jumps and then lets it go as it gets to the next jump.

It is perfectly possible to drive an obstacle course successfully with the reins held in the left hand in the 'English' fashion, but it is a

(above left) Negotiating the 'L' in the obstacle phase at the World Championships, 1986, Ascot. *(Findlay Davidson)*

(above right) The pony team in the obstacle phase at the International Driving Event, Royal Windsor Horse Show.

great deal easier to drive accurately while holding the reins two-handed as I have already described. Indeed most of the course can probably be driven without taking a loop in the leader reins but as with practice it is so easily and so quickly done it is really much better to take a loop in order to bring the leaders round smoothly in front of the wheelers. If you don't take a loop the wheelers and leaders are inclined to turn together producing a left or right 'incline' which doesn't look very good and it also makes it more difficult to settle the team into a straight

line before going through the next pair of cones. It also means that the leaders are forever rushing from side to side trying to get back in front of the wheelers.

It is, of course, vital to know the rules for each of the competitions and in the obstacle driving such points as not crossing the start line before the bell, and crossing the finishing line between the markers, are most important. Under the pressure of circumstances the simplest things tend to be forgotten.

CHAPTER 14

ORGANISING AN EVENT

The first rule is to make certain that you have all the relevant paper work. The following are essential:

1. The latest edition of the FEI Rules for Driving Events (changed in the odd year before the Olympic Games and published at the beginning of the following year).

2. The latest edition of the FEI General Regulations.

3. The latest edition of the FEI Veterinary Regulations. (Both the General and these Regulations are changed in the odd year after the Olympic Games and published at the beginning of the following year.)

4. The FEI Checklist for Organisers for Driving Championships and International Events.

5. The FEI Memorandum for Ground Juries, Technical Delegates, Course Designers and Organisers of International Driving Events.

6. The Combined Driving Rules published by the BHS.

The second rule is to read all these, not very bulky, publications from cover to cover. Some of the points may not appear to be relevant at the time but every word in them has been written as a result of bitter experience and, having read them, the bell will hopefully ring when any unexpected problem arises and the appropriate publication can then be consulted before making a mistake.

One very important point, not covered in so many words, is the need for practice and exercise areas for driven and ridden horses. As far as teams are concerned, four of the horses can be exercised in harness but the fifth horse normally has to be given ridden exercise. Some continentals solve the problem by tying the spare horse to the back of the carriage and exercising it that way.

From the competitor's point of view, the next most vital requirement is good and reliable information, particularly start times and places. Many organisers arrange a 'briefing' session for drivers and their navigators where all the documents can be distributed and announcements made by any or each of the president of the jury, the course designer, the technical delegate, the official vet and the organiser himself. This is not essential but if there is no briefing then the drivers must know where to find all the documents they need, such as programmes, maps of the arena areas, the marathon course, the obstacle driving course, start times and numbers for their carriages. They also need to know where they can find one of the officials, preferably the president of the jury and/or the technical delegate in case they have any questions, and, inevitably, there always are some questions. Experienced drivers develop an eye for unexpected routes through hazards or loopholes in the marking of the marathon course and experienced drivers have also learned that it always pays to ask about doing the unexpected beforehand rather than having to argue about it afterwards.

Dressage arena

There is nothing very mysterious about laying out a dressage arena but it does help if the surface is reasonably smooth and the area fairly flat. It is very difficult to keep up an even rhythm if the team is going up and down hill all the time.

It is essential to have a collecting ring big enough for several teams to move about freely, which means, among other things, that it must be kept clear of spectators. This is just as much in the interest of spectators — and their children, grandparents and dogs — as it is of the drivers.

Marathon course

A team of four horses pulling a purpose built cross-country carriage can go virtually anywhere. The only types of going which are preferably avoided are when there are outcrops of sharp rocks, small tree stumps and deeply rutted tracks which have dried hard. The trouble is that the track width of tractors is not compatible with two horses side by side. One usually has to scramble along the bank in the middle while the other flounders about in one of the tracks, which are usually too narrow for comfort. Even this sort of going is acceptable provided it doesn't go on too long.

Marathon courses are usually quite difficult enough without having to cope with low branches as well. I suspect that course designers are inclined to forget that the driver — and his referee for that matter — sit a lot higher than he does behind the wheel of his Landrover. While the grooms can help to fend off low branches, the driver is virtually helpless as he is likely to have both hands full of reins and has to cope with the whip as well.

There are of course many considerations in laying out a marathon course: finding a convenient circuit without spending too much time on main roads; fitting in the 10 minute halts at appropriate places accessible to support vehicles without interfering with the course; arranging for the hazards to be placed in such a way that spectators can get to them easily without having to follow the course down a narrow track, and finding two reasonably flat, fairly hard and more or less straight stretches of about 1 000 m for the two walks.

The general idea of the whole course is that A is the longest section driven at a modest speed. It is a test of regularity and has the effect of settling the horses for the more demanding sections to follow. The walk in Section B and the 10 minute halt provide a period of rest and recuperation.

Section C is the speed test. The average speed chosen for this section must be balanced against the difficulty of the course. The average team might be able to keep up a steady 20 kph on a straight hard track but only a very fast team could manage that speed on a winding hilly route. However, there is no point in making it possible for the time allowed to be achieved too easily. After all, the object of the competition is to allow the best team to win; it is not intended to allow the average team to get round without penalties.

Section C is relatively short but this cuts both ways as there is not enough time to compensate for the slower parts by going faster in the easy parts, and this needs to be taken into consideration by the course designer.

Section D and the halt again provide for a breather and a chance to prepare for Section E and the hazards. If there is to be a veterinary check at this halt it is important to provide for it to take place where the horses are resting. If the check is to take place somewhere else then the time taken for the check should be added to the 10 minutes of the halt. It is hardly fair on the horses or the grooms to use up part of the 'halt'

time for the veterinary check and then to expect the team to move to another place for what is left of the 10 minute rest period.

Needless to say an abundant supply of water is essential at both halts and the presence of a farrier is desirable. Halts in the vicinity of pubs are always popular both with spectators as well as with drivers, the referees and the back up teams.

Designing hazards is a rapidly developing art but rather like designing the cross-country section of the speed and endurance day of the three-day event, it is quite impossible to predict exactly how each hazard will drive. Even experienced drivers make mistakes and either over or, more frequently, underestimate the problems of hazards.

The aim of the course designer should be to provide a variety of problems in a variety of materials. In addition he should of course aim to place the hazards in such a way that spectators can get from one to the other fairly easily. In theory the solution would be to arrange the course in a series of loops so that the hazards are grouped more or less centrally and fairly close to each other while the course between the hazards takes the drivers on loops into the country. Obviously this is the ideal solution and there are many situations where such a plan could not be achieved. Even so, if the hazards cannot be spread fairly evenly along the whole length of the section, it is still not desirable to bunch them all into the last couple of kilometres.

Design of hazards

In principle the design of individual hazards should be such that no driver is compelled to take a route through the hazard which poses a problem of more than average difficulty. In other words for every tight corner there ought to be an escape route. This is for two reasons: first, so that drivers, who know that such a corner presents the particular team with a real risk of getting stuck, can plan an alternative easier but obviously longer route. Secondly, so that those drivers who are prepared to take the risk can extricate themselves if they fail to make it. Nothing causes more disruption to an event than a team stuck in a hazard in such a way that they end up by breaking it or so that it has to be dismantled. Escape routes, alternative routes or room to loop do not make the hazard any less spectacular for spectators, in fact they make them more interesting as each driver will do them slightly differently and the really good driver will be able to demonstrate his skills even more effectively.

In order to illustrate these points a series of sketches of actual hazards are shown from Windsor 1980 and Zug 1981 on pages 103 and 104.

There are several further factors that need to be borne in mind in the design of hazards. It is very difficult to back a team uphill or in soft sand or deep mud, so consequently it must be assumed that critical turns in such conditions may well cause long hold-ups. If a driver gets stuck by taking the short route when there is plenty of room to loop, he only has himself to blame.

Most purpose built cross-country carriages can be dragged through any gap the horses can get through but there are two absolute limitations. Horses can go sideways and if a post or a tree gets between the back end of a wheeler and up against the splinter bar, the carriage gets stuck. Even angled fenders from the splinter bar to the front wheel can only cope with a glancing blow and then only at the outer end of the splinter bar.

Secondly, any hazard which incorporates logs lying on the ground or large trees or tree stumps with well-developed root branches can cause serious trouble. A front wheel can get trapped in the slot between root branches or it can come up against the square end of a log. The reason is that such obstructions, unlike upright posts, come below the level of any normal fender or bumper bar that can be fitted to a carriage. Any fender fitted much below the level of the splinter bar is liable to catch the wheeler's hind legs. Logs have the added disadvantage that they are not easily visible from the box seat and unless they are really substantial the horses are quite capable of climbing over them.

There has been a lot of discussion about what should be the minimum width between two obstructions in a hazard. The ultimate limiting factor is the width of two horses but in practice the track width of horse carriages is seldom less than 130–140 cm. However, the trouble is that it is unusual to be able to go through a gap at right angles. If the hazard demands that the team must be driven through a 3 m gap at a sharp angle the effective gap can easily be reduced to,

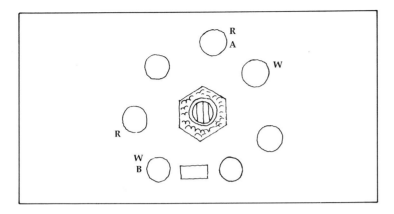

Hazard 1: The Grouse Barrel Garden. *Time allowed 30 seconds.*

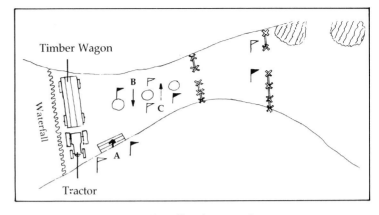

Hazard 3: Virginia Water. *Time allowed 36 seconds.*

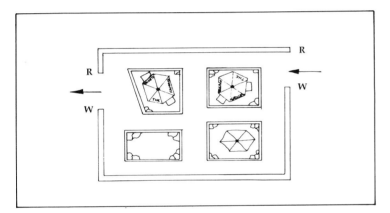

Hazard 6: The Garden Pens. *Time allowed 25 seconds.*

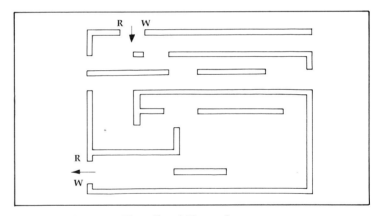

Hazard 8: The Maze. *Time allowed 50 seconds.*

say, 150 cm. The International Rules specify a minimum width of 200 cm, but in certain circumstances, this would be unrealistically narrow.

Obstacle course

The course for the obstacle driving competition should not present too many problems but, as with the construction of show-jumping courses, turns and distances can make all the difference.

Here again the aim should be to vary the course in such a way that some parts need to be driven slowly and carefully while others can be done more quickly. In principle any two pairs of cones within 20 m of each other and on the circumference of a circle with a diameter of 15 m between the inside cones is just about as tight as an average team can manage. Equally it is

Hazards at the World Carriage Driving Championships, Windsor Great Park, September 1980.

⊢ White flag
► Red flag
W = white   R = red

barely possible to get a team to turn from a right-handed circle of 20 m diameter to a left-hand circle of the same diameter where the two pairs of cones are 20 m apart. In order to produce a free flowing course there needs to be a reasonable amount of room to change direction between one pair of cones and the next.

The rules lay down that there must be at least 20 m between pairs of cones. In practice it is as well to allow one team length straight after a pair of cones, about one length for the turn and one length straight before the next pair, that is about 30 m, provided, of course, that the team only has to turn in one direction. If it has to

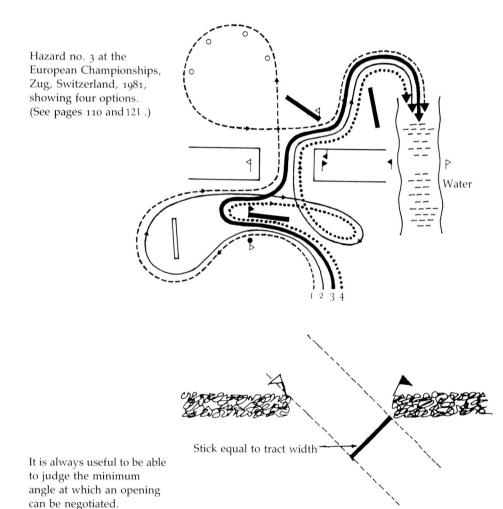

Hazard no. 3 at the European Championships, Zug, Switzerland, 1981, showing four options. (See pages 110 and 121.)

Water

Wall

In order to get through a narrow gap from a narrow lane it is necessary to take the leaders past the gap before attempting to get the carriage through.

Stick equal to tract width

It is always useful to be able to judge the minimum angle at which an opening can be negotiated.

'snake' between pairs of cones as when going from one circle to another then a longer distance is needed.

Some organisers believe that by allowing more than 30 cm over the track width between the cones, it will encourage drivers to go faster. It won't, unless there is a special prize for the obstacle driving. Combined driving consists of three separate competitions but the scoring is cumulative so that with five penalties at risk for hitting a cone, all a driver can do to ensure he does not slip any places in the final results is to have a clear round within the time allowed. Going faster brings no benefits. One way of giving a benefit to faster drivers might be to give all competitors ten penalties before they start the obstacle driving and then to deduct half a penalty for every second in which the course is completed less than the time allowed. In other words a round completed 20 seconds

Driving the 'U' shaped obstacle at the World Championships at Apeldoorn, 1982. (*Author's Collection*)

HORSE DRIVING TRIALS

COMPETITOR'S NUMBER		TIME ALLOWED: SECTION A	TIME ALLOWED: SECTION B	TIME ALLOWED: SECTION C	TIME ALLOWED: SECTION D			SECTION E — OBSTACLE PENALTIES										SECTION E — TIME PENALTIES (COURSE) TIME ALLOWED:			TOTAL COMPETITION B	CLASSIFICATION COMPETITION B	CUMULATIVE TOTAL COMPETITIONS A & B
								1	2	3	4	5	6	7	8	TOTAL		REF. PEN.	TOTAL			
	Finish						Time Taken										Finish					
	Start						Time Penalties										Start					
	Time Taken						Other Penalties										Time Taken					
	Penalties						TOTAL										Less Hold-Ups					
	Ref.Pen.															TOTAL HOLD-UPS	Nett					
	TOTAL						Hold Ups										Penalties					
	Finish						Time Taken										Finish					
	Start						Time Penalties										Start					
	Time Taken						Other Penalties										Time Taken					
	Penalties						TOTAL										Less Hold-Ups					
	Ref.Pen.															TOTAL HOLD-UPS	Nett					
	TOTAL						Hold Ups										Penalties					

Example of a score sheet for Competition B.

APPENDIX A   **SCORER**

No.	NAME	A = AI	AII	AI + AII	PLACE	B A	B	C	D	E SECTIONS	REF	1	2	3	4	5	6	7	8 OBSTACLES	TOTAL B	A & B	PLACE	C F	T	TOTAL C	A,B & C	PLACE

Example of a comprehensive score sheet for a complete event.

faster than the time allowed would wipe out those ten extra penalties, irrespective of the number of cones knocked down.

Scoreboards

Throughout the whole event it is vital to get the scores worked out as soon as possible and posted on a big scoreboard. The board should have room for each of the headings under which a competitor can collect penalties. It may seem rather elaborate but the practical advantage is that mistakes are more easily spotted and competitors can compare their own estimates of their scores with those on the board. For

Example of a judging card for Competition C *(top)*. Example of judges dressage card. *(below)*

HORSE DRIVING TRIALS
JUDGING CARD COMPETITION C

CLEAR ROUNDS

Class No. ....

SPEED REQUIRED .... Yards/Metres per Minute

LENGTH OF COURSE .... Yards/Metres

TIME ALLOWED.................... Mins .... Secs

TIME LIMIT ....Mins .... Secs

NOTE: — Competitors' numbers should NOT be filled in by the Show Secretary, but left for the Judge to complete when the Horse/Pony enters the Ring

No																	Name of Competitor	Total Driving Faults	Time Taken	Time Faults	Total Faults	Award

---

The Scale of Marks is as follows:—

10. Excellent	4. Insufficient
9. Very good	3. Fairly bad
8. Good	2. Bad
7. Fairly good	1. Very bad
6. Satisfactory	0. Not performed
5. Sufficient	

FEI DRESSAGE TEST No. 5 (ADVANCED)

COMPETITOR'S NO

....

Time: 10 minutes (for information only)

Errors of course and dismounting of grooms are penalised as follows:—

1st incident .... 5 penalty points
2nd incident .... 10 penalty points
3rd incident .... 15 penalty points
4th incident .... Elimination

No.	MOVEMENTS		TO BE JUDGED	MARK 0 — 10	REMARKS
1.	A	Enter at working trot	Driving on a straight line: standing on the bit: transitions to working trot.		
	X	Halt — salute. Proceed at working trot			
	C	Track to the right			
2.	M	Collected trot	Impulsion, regularity and accuracy of figures		
	MB	10 metres deviation from side.			

example, if a competitor only sees his total for the marathon and it is much more than his estimate, he has no way of knowing where he has gone wrong or possibly where the mistake in the scoring might be. If the breakdown is shown he can spot immediately where the trouble is and after checking his own estimates he can take up that particular point with the jury or the scorers.

I am sure everyone likes a bit of ceremony for the prizegiving but horses can get rather impatient standing about in an arena and organisers should devise a system which gets the competitors in and out of the arena fairly quickly. I have always favoured the arrangement whereby the competitors go out of the arena in the reverse order of the results which allows the winner to go out last with a bit of a flourish.

CHAPTER 15

HORSE SENSE

Anybody who has anything to do with horses is bound to learn, sooner or later, by their own, often bitter, experience what to do and what not to do. Easier, less damaging and less painful by far is to learn from the experience of others. People have been driving and handling horses for a good many centuries so there is a wealth of experience available.

It might well be instructive and possibly entertaining to give case studies of some of the more dramatic incidents that drivers have experienced while practising for or taking part in combined driving events. However, in virtually every case the dramatic part of the incident is the consequence of a mistake, an oversight, something breaking, or a combination of all three.

It is obviously impossible to visualise every likely and unlikely circumstance. The totally unexpected can and frequently does happen, but in principle the art of avoiding accidents and dramatic incidents is anticipation and taking every reasonable precaution against anything going wrong.

One very good reason for learning from the experience of others is that most horses have an extraordinary memory for unpleasant incidents and they seldom get over a nasty fright. After all, they cannot be expected to tell the difference between a nasty experience and a deliberate punishment. Therefore learning from personal experience may well do lasting damage to the horses.

On the other hand it is quite remarkable what they will bear with calmness and patience once they realise that it is part of what they are expected to do. Anyone who has seen a competition for the best trained police horse will understand what I mean. Sudden noises, like shots being fired, waving flags, banging drums, or walking over (dummy) bodies would give an unprepared horse a fit of the horrors from which it would probably never recover, but with the right training, including both rewards and punishments, most horses will not only accept these alarms but may well come to enjoy the whole thing.

It is worth remembering that the horse, in

The horses are calm and stand quite still in spite of trouble behind. Hazard no. 3 at the European Championships, Zug, Switzerland, 1981. (*Author's Collection*)

At the same hazard, another team has to unhitch to get themselves out of trouble. (*Author's Collection*)

spite of having been domesticated for thousands of years, still retains many of the basic instincts and reactions of its wild ancestors. As far as driving is concerned, the two most important characteristics are that when a horse is frightened its first reaction is to try to run away and that when it is angry or frustrated it will kick. However, I must emphasise that, like all sentient beings, every horse has its own unique character and pattern of behaviour. The art of handling horses is therefore very similar to the art of handling children as it depends almost entirely on the ability to sense what is going on in their minds, to anticipate their reactions to situations and to treat them accordingly.

In practice this means trying to anticipate problems and to visualise the likely consequences of actions, errors and omissions.

Barbara Woodhouse, who spent her life training animals, told a marvellous story of how she persuaded her pony to climb a step-ladder into the hay-loft for a bet. Only later did it strike her that she could not get the pony down again.

That is rather a special case of not considering the consequences. Let me give some other examples. Horses in ordinary blinkers have very limited vision and unless you are extremely careful about leading them in or out of stable doors they may well bump into one side or the other and if anything sharp is protruding they may hurt themselves. As a result the next time they will either try to rush out or refuse to go in again unless their bridle is taken off first.

Putting-to is always a critical operation, particularly in the early days, as any fright at this point can cause endless problems in the future. Equally, if the horse has a chance to discover that there is no need to associate putting-to with anything frightening or unpleasant it will eventually put up with minor incidents without a fuss.

If you learn to fly, one of the very first things you will be required to do is to inspect the outside of the aircraft before getting into it and then once installed you will go through a number of check lists culminating with a list of vital actions before take-off. This is standard practice in every aircraft from single-engined single seaters to long distance airliners. Something of the sort would not be at all a bad idea before setting off with a team of horses. In any case an all round inspection when all is ready before getting on the box is always a good idea. The particular points to look for are the reins (they should be correctly fitted and the right way round), the blinkers and bridles, the buckling of the coupling reins, the traces, pole-straps and breechings (if fitted).

A very good rule is never to trust a horse or a team once it is connected to a carriage. By that I don't mean that the horses are less trustworthy, but simply that, as the consequences of anything going wrong are so much more serious when a carriage is involved, it is best to be in a position to stop anything happening instantly. To begin with it may be necessary for the grooms to hold the horses until the driver is ready to move off, but the object should be to teach the horses to stand quietly on their own and it should only be necessary for the grooms to stand close enough

Things can sometimes go wrong. (*Alf. Baker*)

to be able to grab the horses at an instant's notice. Needless to say the horses must always be held if there is no one on the box.

Horses get used to a routine very quickly so that it is important to establish the routine to suit the driver's convenience and to make certain that the horses only react to deliberate signals. For example, if you tell the grooms to 'stand clear' in a loud voice and then put off the brake with a clatter and ask the horses to walk on, the chances are that the next time you do it the horses will move off the moment you speak or touch the brake. Therefore only signal to the grooms to move slowly out of the way by nodding your head, release the brake silently and then get the horses to stand still for varying periods from a few seconds to several minutes before asking them to walk on. Once in a while it is a good idea to back them for a few paces before setting off. It is very unwise to start trotting immediately on departure from the stables except very occasionally and then only with quiet and experienced horses.

During the training of young horses in a team or whenever practising hazards it is always sensible to take two grooms. With an experienced team, other than when doing something unusual, one groom is sufficient. To take out even the most experienced team single-handed is foolhardy.

Some people have no option but to drive along public roads in the traffic. In the normal course of events this should not cause any particular problems for an experienced team but naturally it involves all the risks inherent in modern traffic conditions. Needless to say the sensible thing to do before taking a team into traffic is to get the horses used to traffic first ridden and then driven as a pair.

The one cardinal rule about driving out with a team or a pair is never to try to go in anywhere or up any narrow lane unless you are certain of being able to get out again. If in any doubt always send the groom to reconnoitre before getting into a situation where withdrawal becomes hazardous or impossible without taking the horses out, and leading them back individually. This is not all that easily done by only two people.

Some horses will shy regularly at certain objects no matter how often they see them. Provided it doesn't shy too badly it is tolerable but it must always be anticipated. If a horse shies really badly it can be extremely dangerous. Some can be cured but the sad truth is that the success rate in curing bad shying is not high.

Every now and then a horse will suddenly start behaving in an uncharacteristic, even an irrational manner. Pulling, head-shaking, nagging its neighbour, plunging, refusing to stand still or even trying to lie down are all forms of behaviour that may be signals that something may be wrong with a horse. The first things to check are the mouth and the bars of the jaw for bruising, cuts or general soreness. A change of bit may be all that is needed. However, it is also worth checking the teeth for sharp and irritating edges, and the ears for wax or mites. If nothing unusual is found in those areas get the vet to check the head, the bones in the neck and then the spine. A slight dislocation of a vertebra may well be causing sudden shooting pains which are bound to affect the horse's behaviour.

Probably because carriage horses are not ridden quite so much, they seem to be less liable to lameness. However, it can happen and if a horse should show signs of lameness while being driven, the sooner you can get it home the better, but first check that there is no obvious reason for the lameness such as a cast shoe or a stone wedged between the frog and the shoe or some physical damage around the fetlock or coronet.

If it is necessary, for any reason, to take a bridle off a horse always disconnect the horse from the carriage first. If a horse without a bridle decides to take off with the carriage there is very little anyone can do about it.

On returning to the yard, the driver should remain on the box holding the reins until the grooms are in position at the leaders' and wheelers' heads. The correct sequence for disconnecting the horses is designed to minimise the consequences of anything going wrong during the procedure. On no account should any one of the horses be led away until all of them are completely disconnected from the carriage and from each other.

All these points may seem to be rather trifling or pedantic but doing things in a safe and orderly way is no more difficult than doing them in any other way, and it may well save a great deal of trouble. Unfortunately there is never as much credit to be gained from preventing an accident or disease as there is in curing it. The only satisfaction is that you have been for another outing without incident and for that it is worth taking a lot of trouble.

CHAPTER 16

'I HEAR YOU ARE DOING THIS DANGEROUS CARRIAGE DRIVING THING?'

Driving can have its interesting moments. Several years ago when I was in the process of introducing sedate and unsuspecting Buckingham Palace carriage horses to the surprises and wholly novel demands of driving competitions, I decided they needed a lesson in crossing water. Short of the unlikely possibility of a burst water main in the Mall, they had experienced nothing more daunting in the way of water than an ordinary London street puddle. Somehow I had to persuade them to cross a small stream. They had been ridden across it but that sort of introduction doesn't always mean much to horses whose mentality is sometimes difficult to fanthom. 'Yes', they seem to say, 'we've been ridden across this water but we are not pulling this carriage across it.' I had decided, fortunately as it turned out, to take out one pair at a time. We got to the water's edge and, believing in patience, we just stood there; no amount of cajoling would persuade these two state horses to do anything so undignified as to get their feet wet.

I then suddenly remembered that I had some sugar lumps with me in a jam jar. I used it when I visited the horses in the stables and also as a reward on return from an outing and they had already learnt to recognise the rattle of the lumps in the jar. I sent 'Tommy' Thompson over to the other side of the water to rattle the jar of sugar. This produced quite an encouraging reaction and it was obvious that the greedier of the two was prepared to sacrifice his dignity for a lump of sugar. Quite suddenly he set off into the water and the other started forward from force of habit.

Unfortunately the more timid of the two quickly realised it had been 'had', so it tried to stop, but the other one went on, with the result that the carriage swung sharply downstream and headed for the arch of a bridge barely large enough to admit a swan. At this point I had the distinct impression that the stream was not wide enough to allow the carriage to turn round and it was obvious — even to the horses — that the banks were too steep to climb. As it happened I had offered to take an unsuspecting weekend guest for a drive that morning and out of the corner of my eye I could see his face assuming a look of considerable alarm. The impression was confirmed by the whiteness of his knuckles as he clutched the rail beside his seat.

I am not conscious that I actually took any action to get out of this predicament. I can only suspect that the greedier horse had eventually realised that it was heading away from the sugar and getting its feet wet to no purpose, so it simply turned about and walked up to where Tommy was still rattling the sugar. As I say, I think that is what happened, as my eyes were shut at the time waiting for the inevitable crack as the pole broke. I will never know why it didn't.

Later in the training process I took a team to Sandringham and as there was no suitable water crossing I had a rudimentary ford bulldozed across a drainage ditch in a water meadow, which was not a sensible thing to do. By this time the horses were prepared to go through water, but what I did not realise was that the bottom of the ditch was a good deal softer than it appeared. The leaders floundered a bit but got through, but just as the wheelers got to the water the front wheels of the carriage sank into the mud, whereupon the wheelers gave a great heave and broke all four of their traces, leaving the reins as the only connection between me and them.

The next thing I knew I was lying on the far side of the ditch looking back at Tommy still sitting on the box of the now abandoned carriage with a look of total disbelief on his face. This didn't last long as four large carriage horses were careering around the meadow spraying bits of harness as they went. One of them made for the gate and disappeared down the track for home. As luck would have it, coming the other way was a very surprised daughter on a young event horse, who gallantly rode to father's rescue.

Water played quite a large part in the 1975 European Championships at the Baltic resort of Sopot in Poland. The course took us across a beach and then into about a foot of water under the local pier. Needless to say, my horses had not experienced the seaside before so I decided to introduce them to this phenomenon in pairs. I got down to the beach all right but as soon as we got into the soft sand at the back of the beach, that was enough for them. This was rather an embarrassing situation as scantily clad comrades of indeterminate sex watched impassively from the picnic sites as these two crazy fully grown foreigners tried to persuade two large horses to pull their damned carriage through the sand. By both of us working on the spokes of the wheels we got it going again and all was well. I was a little more careful with the other pair and gradually got them used to the very soft sand before trying to cross the beach to the sea.

Eventually I took the team down and we got through the sand all right, but now I had to get them to face the indescribable horrors of the very small breaking waves. My track along the beach described a series of graceful arcs as they followed the retreating wave and then sidled up the beach again as the next wave came in. Nothing I could do would make them paddle along in the shallow water.

True to the incomprehensible equine thought processes, on the day they went straight into the water and under the pier as if it were a regular feature of the Opening of Parliament procession.

A sort of woodland pond also featured in, I think it was, Section E of the Sopot course. On the reconnaissance of the course all the competitors were stopped at this pond to watch a demonstration by a pair of horses being driven through it. In spite of the fact that the cart had pneumatic tyres I noticed that at one point it fairly leapt into the air, nearly spilling the driver. Everyone seemed to be quite satisfied about the depth but I was a bit suspicious about the bumps and later on I came back to the scene on my own, or almost on my own as I was being followed by a carload of police. I am not quite sure what went through their minds as they saw me taking off first my shoes and socks and then my trousers before wading into the pond clad in a shirt. It didn't take me long to find the cause of the bump: there were two very large rocks lying on the otherwise sandy bottom. A word with the course designer settled the problem promptly and two rocks about the size of the Stone of Scone probably still repose gracefully at the water's edge.

I have twice made an involuntary descent from the box seat. I went round a corner on a slope a bit too quickly at Lowther one year and

went out of the side door. Fortunately I was able to hold on to the reins and the horses stopped. However, the two grooms were off and away like lightning leaving the referee the sole occupant of the carriage. It was fairly obvious by his expression that this was not the sort of behaviour he had come to expect.

It may have been that this story got around the referees' 'union' but on one occasion coming down that famous hill opposite Mellerstain House, the grass was rather wet and I had a horse that insisted on pulling downhill as well as under all other conditions. With my foot hard on the ineffective brakes and hauling on the reins I suddenly noticed a void beside me where the referee should have been. When I enquired what had happened I was told he had jumped off but was now standing on the back step. He apologised afterwards — quite unnecessarily as I would have done the same thing if I hadn't had the reins in my hands.

Now that carriages are built lower and with a lower centre of gravity, turning over is not quite such a hazard as it used to be, but I have experienced this undignified process on two occasions. As the incidents illustrate the consequences of improved techniques in carriage construction, I will describe them both.

Years ago I competed at Lowther with the old wooden 'Balmoral Dogcart'. The hazard required the team to be driven round a very large stump which stuck up above the ground some two

(*opposite page*) Under the pier at Sopot, 1975 . (*Zbigniew Kosycarz*)

feet, and sticking out round about its circum-ference were some particularly vicious root branches. The inevitable happened. The inside front wheel got caught between two roots and rode up the stump and over we went with a quite impressive splintering crash, and the horses were gone, breaking traces and wooden swingle-trees like cotton and match wood, and the carriage was out of action for months.

Some years later I was competing in Hungary and I had the mortifying experience of turning over in the only hazard in which no other com-petitor incurred any penalties at all. But this time I had a metal-framed carriage, metal pole and metal swingle-trees. The cause of the upset was a combination of a pulling leader (the same one as at Mellerstain − needless to say), a very solidly constructed structure rather like a 'wigwam' and two huge long-horned Hungarian cattle. I am sure they were bulls, but I didn't have time to look.

Anyway, the leader saw these vast crea-tures − with horns as long as Highlanders − and pulled the whole team into the wigwam, and of course the wheels rode up the sloping side and over we went, with me landing on top of the famous former World Champion Imre Abonyi, who was my referee. This time I hung on to the reins, lying on my back, the grooms were away in a flash and the horses stopped. The only damage was a broken splash board and the hook on the end of the pole which had been pulled out straight. We pushed the carriage upright and, by holding all parts of the carriage and horses together, we walked through the rest of the hazard. Once outside the penalty zone, we bent the hook more or less back into position, hooked on the swingle-trees and continued.

I am absolutely convinced that but for the new carriage and the metal pole and swingle-trees, we would still be looking for the horses on the plains of central Hungary.

The occasion that converted me to metal swingle-trees was the World Championships in Apeldoorn in Holland in 1976. The first bar went as we drove into some soft sand in Section A. I was not able to do much about it as I had been thrown out by a bump, but fortunately the grooms got to the horses very quickly and stopped them.

The next pair of lead bars went when we drove over a clattering wooden bridge. The wheelers thought nothing of it but with that infallible equine logic the leaders appeared to argue 'Yes, we've clattered over the bridge but we can't stand that dreadful noise behind us' − and they were off. We just sat there with the pair of wheelers looking as if it were the most natural thing in the world to be abandoned by the leaders on a track deep in a Dutch wood. We watched in considerable apprehension as the two lunatics careered off into the forest, hoping they wouldn't wrap themselves round a tree and wondering how on earth we were going to find them before they tried to board the ferry at the Hook of Holland. Then to our amazement they turned round and careered back towards us and one of them considerately tripped over a stump and fell virtually at our feet. Throughout this whole episode their reins had remained intact and they hadn't even broken the connecting strap, so we used up the last of our spare bars, put them to and went on.

It wasn't quite the end of the story because, in order to reconnect the leaders more easily and to get clear of the course I cut through some trees, leaving out about 20 yards of the course. I was consequently reported to have 'deviated' from the course in spite of the fact that I had not missed a turning flag. Oddly enough the whole thing happened so quickly that I still managed to keep ahead of the next following competitor. The last remaining bars went in another patch of soft sand so we finished the course with the leaders attached to the wheelers by halter ropes. Even after all these frustrating incidents I didn't come in last, in fact I was 20th out of 30.

Another example of the advantages of less breakable materials was at the 1981 National Championships at Windsor. Hazard no. 6 consisted of a large tree in the middle with three substantial logs placed fairly close around it.

HRH The Duke of Edinburgh and the team of bays successfully negotiating hazard no. 3 at the European Championships, Zug, Switzerland, 1981, despite the number. (*Author's Collection*)

This hazard caused a lot of trouble but needless to say I managed to find a unique way of getting stuck. I caught the off front wheel against the end of the log at gate C. It was obvious that I'd be there for ages if I didn't get the grooms down and with their help we were out very quickly. When we got out we realised that the pole had been bent at least 30° to the left. All we could do was to scramble along the track between the bushes to the next clearing before stopping to decide what to do. With the pole so badly bent there was no hope of going on. However, we thought we would try to bend it straight so I drove the carriage up to a tree in such a way that the off front wheel was lying against it. The grooms then hauled the wheelers across to the right and it worked, the pole bent back again, only not quite straight as I was a bit anxious it might be a bit fatigued after all the bangs and bumps of a couple of seasons, and break off. Anyway, it got us through the sandpit but sadly it contributed to a hang up in the last hazard from which I only managed to escape with 30 seconds to spare before being eliminated.

I always seem to come back to water, in spite of the fact that, as far as competitions are concerned, I have never had any serious problems. Perhaps it was this luck that saved me at Holker one year. Having just narrowly negotiated the last hazard before reaching the water I was greeted by an agitated judge informing me that the last three competitors had turned over in the water. I am sure it was meant well but it is hardly the sort of news likely to inspire confidence and calm. In the event they went through without a twitch.

People often say to me 'I hear you are doing this dangerous carriage driving thing'. There have been a few accidents and injuries but, considering the number of drivers and the number of events and the fact that it is still a relatively new sport, I would certainly not describe it as dangerous. In any case, what is dangerous? Ther are some people who are not to be trusted with a bicycle. Exciting, yes; rewarding, yes; but dangerous, no. That is, not if done sensibly and if the proper safeguards and precautions are observed.

RECOMMENDED READING

Breaking and Training the Driving Horse by Doris Ganton (Wilshire, USA, 1984)

Harnessing Up by Anne Norris & Nancy Pethick (J.A. Allen, 1979)

Manual of Coaching by Fairman Rogers (Lippincott, USA, 1900)

Driving Lessons by Edwin Howlett (Russell, USA, 1894)

On the Box Seat by Tom Ryder (Horse Drawn Carriages, 1970)

Hints on Driving by Captain C. Morley Knight (J.A. Allen, 1969)

The Driving Book by Major H. Faudel-Phillips (Waltham Cross, 1943)

The Encyclopaedia of Carriage Driving by Sallie Walrond (J.A. Allen, 1988)

Looking at Carriages by Sallie Walrond (J.A. Allen, 1992)

A Guide to Driving Horses by Sallie Walrond (Nelson, 1971)

Driving by Francis Ware & Others (Heinemann, 1904)

The Coach Horse by Stanley Jepsen (Barnes, USA, 1977)

Training the Driving Pony by Allan Conder (Arco, USA, 1977)

Harness by John Philipson (A. Reid, 1882)

The Harness Horse by Sir Walter Gilbey (Vinton, 1898)

Saddlery and Harness Making by Paul N. Hasluck (J.A. Allen, 1962)

Art of Driving by Max Pape (J.A. Allen, 1982)

Combined Driving by Emil Bernard Jung (Privately printed, 1987)

INDEX